LADY AUDLEY'S SECRET.

BY

M. E. BRADDON,

AUTHOR OF "AURORA FLOYD."

IN THREE VOLUMES.

VOL. I.

EIGHTH EDITION REVISED

LONDON:

TINSLEY BROS., 18, CATHERINE STREET, STRAND.

1862.

CONTENTS.

——◆——

LADY AUDLEY'S SECRET.

CHAPTER I.

LUCY.

It lay low down in a hollow, rich with fine old timber and luxuriant pastures; and you came upon it through an avenue of limes, bordered on either side by meadows, over the high hedges of which the cattle looked inquisitively at you as you passed, wondering, perhaps, what you wanted; for there was no thoroughfare, and unless you were going to the Court you had no business there at all.

At the end of this avenue there was an old arch and a clock-tower, with a stupid, bewildering clock, which had only one hand; and which

jumped straight from one hour to the next, and
was therefore always in extremes. Through this
arch you walked straight into the gardens of
Audley Court.

A smooth lawn lay before you, dotted with
groups of rhododendrons, which grew in more
perfection here than anywhere else in the county.
To the right there were the kitchen gardens, the
fish-pond, and an orchard bordered by a dry
moat, and a broken ruin of a wall, in some places
thicker than it was high, and everywhere overgrown with trailing ivy, yellow stonecrop, and
dark moss.   To the left there was a broad
gravelled walk, down which, years ago, when
the place had been a convent, the quiet nuns
had walked hand in hand; a wall bordered with
espaliers, and shadowed on one side by goodly
oaks, which shut out the flat landscape, and
circled in the house and gardens with a darkening shelter.

The house faced the arch, and occupied three
sides of a quadrangle.   It was very old, and
very irregular and rambling. The windows were

uneven; some small, some large, some with heavy stone mullions and rich stained glass; others with frail lattices that rattled in every breeze; others so modern that they might have been added only yesterday. Great piles of chimneys rose up here and there behind the pointed gables, and seemed as if they were so broken down by age and long service, that they must have fallen but for the straggling ivy which, crawling up the walls and trailing even over the roof, wound itself about them and supported them. The principal door was squeezed into a corner of aturret at one angle of the building, as if it was in hiding from dangerous visitors, and wished to keep itself a secret—a noble door for all that—old oak, and studded with great square-headed iron nails, and so thick that the sharp iron knocker struck upon it with a muffled sound; and the visitor rang a clanging bell that dangled in a corner amongst the ivy, lest the noise of the knocking should never penetrate the stronghold.

A glorious old place—a place that visitors fell into raptures with; feeling a yearning wish to

have done with life, and to stay there for ever,
staring into the cool fish-ponds, and counting. the
bubbles as the roach and carp rose to the surface
of the water—a spot in which Peace seemed to
have taken up her abode, setting her soothing
hand on every tree and flower; on the still ponds
and quiet alleys; the shady corners of the old-
fashioned rooms; the deep window-seats behind
the painted glass; the low meadows and the
stately avenues—ay, even upon the stagnant well,
which, cool and sheltered as all else in the old
place, hid itself away in a shrubbery behind the
gardens, with an idle handle that was never
turned, and a lazy rope so rotten that the pail
had broken away from it, and had fallen into the
water.

A noble place; inside as well as out, a noble
place—a house in which you incontinently lost
yourself if ever you were so rash as to go about
it alone; a house in which no one room had
any sympathy with another, every chamber running off at a tangent into an inner chamber,
and through that down some narrow staircase

leading to a door which, in its turn, led back
into that very part of the house from which you
thought yourself the farthest; a house that could
never have been planned by any mortal architect, but must have been the handiwork of that
good old builder—Time, who, adding a room one
year, and knocking down a room another year,
toppling over now a chimney coeval with the
Plantagenets, and setting up one in the style of
the Tudors; shaking down a bit of Saxon wall
there, and allowing a Norman arch to stand
here; throwing in a row of high narrow windows
in the reign of Queen Anne, and joining on a
dining-room after the fashion of the time of
Hanoverian George I. to a refectory that had
been standing since the Conquest, had contrived,
in some eleven centuries, to run up such a
mansion as was not elsewhere to be met with
throughout the county of Essex. Of course, in
such a house, there were secret chambers: the
little daughter of the present owner, Sir Michael
Audley, had fallen by accident upon the discovery of one. A board had rattled under her

feet in the great nursery where she played, and
on attention being drawn to it, it was found to
be loose, and so removed, revealing a ladder
leading to a hiding-place between the floor of the
nursery and the ceiling of the room below—a
hiding-place so small that he who hid there must
have crouched on his hands and knees or lain at
full length, and yet large enough to contain a
quaint old carved oak chest half filled with
priests' vestments which had been hidden away,
no doubt, in those cruel days when the life of a
man was in danger if he was discovered to have
harboured a Roman Catholic priest, or to have
had mass said in his house.

The broad outer moat was dry and grass-
grown, and the laden trees of the orchard hung
over it with gnarled straggling branches that
drew fantastical patterns upon the green slope.
Within this moat there was, as I have said, the
fish-pond—a sheet of water that extended the
whole length of the garden, and bordering which
there was an avenue called the lime-tree walk;
an avenue so shaded from the sun and sky, so

screened from observation by the thick shelter of the over-arching trees, that it seemed a chosen place for secret meetings or for stolen interviews; a place in which a conspiracy might have been planned or a lover's vow registered with equal safety; and yet it was scarcely twenty paces from the house.

At the end of this dark arcade there was the shrubbery, where, half buried amongst the tangled branches and the neglected weeds, stood the rusty wheel of that old well of which I have spoken. It had been of good service in its time, no doubt; and busy nuns have perhaps drawn the cool water with their own fair hands; but it had fallen with disuse now, and scarcely any one at Audley Court knew whether the spring had dried up or not. But sheltered as was the solitude of this lime-tree walk, I doubt very much if it was ever put to any romantic uses. Often in the cool of the evening Sir Michael Audley would stroll up and down smoking his cigar, with his dog at his heels, and his pretty young wife dawdling by his side; but in about ten minutes the baronet

and his companion would grow tired of the rustling limes and the still water, hidden under the
spreading leaves of the water-lilies, and the long
green vista with the broken well at the end, and
would stroll back to the white drawing-room,
where my lady played dreamy melodies by
Beethoven and Mendelssohn till her husband
fell asleep in his easy chair.

Sir Michael Audley was fifty-six years of age,
and he had married a second wife three months
after his fifty-fifth birthday. He was a big man,
tall and stout, with a deep sonorous voice, handsome black eyes, and a white beard—a white
beard which made him look venerable against his
will, for he was as active as a boy, and one of
the hardest riders in the county.   For seventeen
years he had been a widower with an only child, a
daughter, Alicia Audley, now eighteen, and by no
means too well pleased at having a step-mother
brought home to the Court; for Miss Alicia had
reigned supreme in her father's house since her
earliest childhood, and had carried the keys, and
jingled them in the pockets of her silk aprons,

and lost them in the shrubbery, and dropped them into the pond, and given all manner of trouble about them from the hour in which she entered her teens, and had on that account deluded herself into the sincere belief that for the whole of that period she had been keeping house.

But Miss Alicia's day was over; and now, when she asked anything of the housekeeper, the house-keeper would tell her that she would speak to my lady, or she would consult my lady, and if my lady pleased it should be done. So the baronet's daughter, who was an excellent horsewoman and a very clever artist, spent most of her time out of doors, riding about the green lanes, and sketching the cottage children, and the ploughboys, and the cattle, and all manner of animal life that came in her way. She set her face with a sulky determination against any intimacy between her-self and the baronet's young wife; and amiable as that lady was, she found it quite impossible to overcome Miss Alicia's prejudices and dislike; or to convince the spoilt girl that she had not done her a cruel injury in marrying Sir Michael Audley.

The truth was that Lady Audley had, in becoming the wife of Sir Michael, made one of those apparently advantageous matches which are apt to draw upon a woman the envy and hatred of her sex. She had come into the neighbourhood as a governess in the family of a surgeon in the village near Audley Court. No one knew anything of her except that she came in answer to an advertisement which Mr. Dawson, the surgeon, had inserted in the *Times*. She came from London ; and the only reference she gave was to a lady at a school at Brompton, where she had once been a teacher. But this reference was so satisfactory that none other was needed, and Miss Lucy Graham was received by the surgeon as the instructress of his daughters. Her accomplishments were so brilliant and numerous, that it seemed strange that she should have answered an advertisement offering such very moderate terms of remuneration as those named by Mr. Dawson : but Miss Graham seemed perfectly well satisfied with her situation, and she taught the girls to play sonatas by Beethoven, and to paint from

Nature after Creswick, and walked through the dull, out-of-the-way village to the humble little church three times on Sunday, as contentedly as if she had no higher aspiration in the world than to do so all the rest of her life.

People who observed this accounted for it by saying that it was part of her amiable and gentle nature always to be light-hearted, happy, and contented under any circumstances.

Wherever she went she seemed to take joy and brightness with her. In the cottages of the poor her fair face shone like a sunbeam. She would sit for a quarter of an hour talking to some old woman, and apparently as pleased with the admiration of a toothless crone as if she had been listening to the compliments of a marquis; and when she tripped away, leaving nothing behind her (for her poor salary gave no scope to her benevolence), the old woman would burst out into senile raptures with her grace, her beauty, and her kindliness, such as she never bestowed upon the vicar's wife, who half fed and clothed her. For you see Miss Lucy Graham was blessed

with that magic power of fascination by which a
woman can charm with a word or intoxicate with
a smile. Every one loved, admired, and praised
her. The boy who opened the five-barred gate
that stood in her pathway ran home to his mother
to tell of her pretty looks, and the sweet voice in
which she thanked him for the little service. The
verger at the church who ushered her into the
surgeon's pew; the vicar who saw the soft blue
eyes uplifted to his face as he preached his simple
sermon; the porter from the railway-station who
brought her sometimes a letter or a parcel, and
who never looked for reward from her; her
employer; his visitors; her pupils; the servants;
everybody, high and low, united in declaring that
Lucy Graham was the sweetest girl that ever
lived.

Perhaps it was this cry which penetrated into
the quiet chambers of Audley Court; or perhaps
it was the sight of her pretty face, looking over
the surgeon's high pew every Sunday morning.
However it was, it was certain that Sir Michael
Audley suddenly experienced a strong desire

to be better acquainted with Mr. Dawson's
governess.

He had only to hint this to the worthy doctor
for a little party to be got up, to which the vicar
and his wife, and the baronet and his daughter,
were invited.

That one quiet evening sealed Sir Michael's
fate. He could no more resist the tender fascination of those soft and melting blue eyes; the
graceful beauty of that slender throat and droop-
ing head, with its wealth of showering flaxen
curls; the low music of that gentle voice; the
perfect harmony which pervaded every charm,
and made all doubly charming in this woman;
than he could resist his destiny. Destiny! Why,
she was his destiny! He had never loved before.
What had been his marriage with Alicia's mother
but a dull, jog-trot bargain, made to keep some
estate in the family that would have been just as
well out of it? What had been his love for his
first wife but a poor, pitiful, smouldering spark,
too dull to be extinguished, too feeble to burn?
But *this* was love—this fever, this longing, this

restless, uncertain, miserable hesitation; these cruel fears that his age was an insurmountable barrier to his happiness; this sick hatred of his white beard; this frenzied wish to be young again, with glistening raven hair, and a slim waist, such as he had had twenty years before; these wakeful nights and melancholy days, so gloriously brightened if he chanced to catch a glimpse of her sweet face behind the window curtains as he drove past the surgeon's house; all these signs gave token of the truth; and told only too plainly that, at the sober age of fifty-five, Sir Michael Audley had fallen ill of the terrible fever called love.

I do not think that throughout his courtship the baronet once calculated upon his wealth or his position as a strong reason for his success. If he ever remembered these things, he dismissed the thought of them with a shudder. It pained him too much to believe for a moment that any one so lovely and innocent could value herself against a splendid house or a good old title. No; his hope was that as her life had been most likely one of toil and dependence, and as she was very young (nobody exactly knew her age, but she looked little more than twenty), she might never have formed any attachment, and that he, being the first to woo her, might by tender attentions, by generous watchfulness, by a love which should recall to her the father she had lost, and by a protecting care that should make him necessary to her, win her young heart, and obtain from her fresh and earliest love alone the promise of her hand.   It was a very romantic day dream, no doubt ; but, for all that, it seemed in a very fair way to be realised.   Lucy Graham appeared by no means to dislike the baronet's attentions. There was nothing whatever in her manner of the shallow artifice employed by a woman who wishes to captivate a rich man.   She was so used to admiration from every one, high and low, that Sir Michael's conduct made very little impression upon her.   Again, he had been so many years a widower that people had given up the idea of his ever marrying again.   At last, however, Mrs. Dawson spoke to the governess on the subject.

The surgeon's wife was sitting in the school-room busy at work, while Lucy was putting the finishing touches to some water-coloured sketches done by her pupils.

" Do you know, my dear Miss Graham," said Mrs. Dawson, " I think you ought to consider yourself a remarkably lucky girl."

The governess lifted her head from its stooping attitude, and stared wonderingly at her employer, shaking back a shower of curls. They were the most wonderful curls in the world—soft and feathery, always floating away from her face, and making a pale halo round her head when the sunlight shone through them.

" What do you mean, my dear Mrs. Dawson ? " she asked, dipping her camel's-hair brush into the wet aquamarine upon the palette, and poising it carefully before putting in the delicate streak of purple which was to brighten the horizon in her pupil's sketch.

" Why, I mean, my dear, that it only rests with yourself to become Lady Audley, and the mistress of Audley Court."

Lucy Graham dropped the brush upon the picture, and flushed scarlet to the roots of her fair hair; and then grew pale again, far paler than Mrs. Dawson had ever seen her before.

"My dear, don't agitate yourself," said the surgeon's wife, soothingly; "you know that nobody asks you to marry Sir Michael unless you wish. Of course it would be a magnificent match; he has a splendid income, and is one of the most generous of men. Your position would be very high, and you would be enabled to do a great deal of good; but, as I said before, you must be entirely guided by your own feelings. Only one thing I must say, and that is, that if Sir Michael's attentions are not agreeable to you, it is really scarcely honourable to encourage him."

"His attentions—encourage him!" muttered Lucy, as if the words bewildered her. "Pray, pray don't talk to me, Mrs. Dawson. I had no idea of this. It is the last thing that would have occurred to me." She leaned her elbows on the drawing-board before her, and clasping her hands over her face, seemed for some minutes to be thinking deeply. She wore a narrow black ribbon round her neck, with a locket or a cross, or a miniature, perhaps, attached to it; but whatever the trinket was, she always kept it hidden under her dress. Once or twice, while she sat silently thinking, she removed one of her hands from before her face, and fidgeted nervously with the ribbon, clutching at it with a half-angry gesture, and twisting it backwards and forwards between her fingers.

"I think some people are born to be unlucky, Mrs. Dawson," she said, by-and-by; "it would be a great deal too much good fortune for me to become Lady Audley."

She said this with so much bitterness in her tone, that the surgeon's wife looked up at her with surprise.

"You unlucky, my dear!" she exclaimed. "I think you're the last person who ought to talk like that—you, such a bright, happy creature, that it does every one good to see you. I'm sure I don't know what we shall do if Sir Michael robs us of you."

After this conversation they often spoke upon the subject, and Lucy never again showed any emotion whatever when the baronet's admiration for her was canvassed. It was a tacitly understood thing in the surgeon's family that whenever Sir Michael proposed, the governess would quietly accept him; and, indeed, the simple Dawsons would have thought it something more than madness in a penniless girl to reject such an offer.

So one misty June evening Sir Michael, sitting opposite to Lucy Graham at a window in the surgeon's little drawing-room, took an opportunity, while the family happened by some accident to be absent from the room, of speaking upon the subject nearest to his heart. He made the governess in few but solemn words an offer of his hand. There was something almost touching in the manner and tone in which he spoke to her—half in deprecation, knowing that he could hardly expect to be the choice of a beautiful young girl, and praying rather that she would reject him, even though she broke his heart by doing so, than that she should accept his offer if she did not love him.

"I scarcely think there is a greater sin, Lucy," he said solemnly, "than that of the woman who marries a man she does not love. You are so precious to me, my beloved, that deeply as my heart is set on this, and bitter as the mere thought of disappointment is to me, I would not have you commit such a sin for any happiness of mine. If my happiness could be achieved by such an act, which it could not—which it never could," he repeated earnestly, "nothing but misery can result from a marriage dictated by any motive but truth and love."

Lucy Graham was not looking at Sir Michael, but straight out into the misty twilight and the dim landscape far away beyond the little garden. The baronet tried to see her face, but her profile was turned to him, and he could not discover the expression of her eyes. If he could have done so, he would have seen a yearning gaze which seemed as if it would have pierced the far obscurity and looked away—away into another world.

" Lucy, you heard me ?"

" Yes," she said gravely; not coldly, or in any way as if she were offended at his words.

" And your answer ?"

She did not remove her gaze from the darkening country side, but for some moments was quite silent; then turning to him with a sudden passion in her manner, that lighted up her face with a new and wonderful beauty which the baronet perceived even in the growing twilight, she fell on her knees at his feet.

" No, Lucy; no, no !" he cried vehemently, " not here, not here ! "

" Yes, here, here," she said, the strange passion which agitated her making her voice sound shrill and piercing—not loud, but preternaturally distinct; " here, and nowhere else. How good you are—how noble and how generous ! Love you ! Why there are women a hundred times my superiors in beauty and in goodness who might love you dearly; but you ask too much of me. You ask too much of *me !* Remember what my life has been; only remember that. From my

very babyhood I have never seen anything but
poverty. My father was a gentleman; clever,
accomplished, generous, handsome—but poor.
My mother——But do not let me speak of her.
Poverty, poverty, trials, vexations, humiliations,
deprivations! *You* cannot tell; you, who are
amongst those for whom life is so smooth and
easy; you can never guess what is endured by
such as we. Do not ask too much of me, then.
I *cannot* be disinterested; I cannot be blind to
the advantages of such an alliance. I cannot,
I cannot!"

Beyond her agitation and her passionate vehemence, there was an undefined something in her
manner which filled the baronet with a vague
alarm. She was still on the ground at his feet,
crouching rather than kneeling, her thin white
dress clinging about her, her pale hair streaming
over her shoulders, her great blue eyes glittering in
the dusk, and her hands clutching at the black
ribbon about her throat, as if it had been strang-
ling her.

"Don't ask too much of me," she kept

repeating; "I have been selfish from my baby-hood."

"Lucy, Lucy, speak plainly. Do you dislike me?"

"Dislike you! No, no!"

"But is there any one else whom you love?"

She laughed aloud at his question. "I do not love any one in the world," she answered.

He was glad of her reply; and yet that and the strange laugh jarred upon his feelings. He was silent for some moments, and then said with a kind of effort,—

"Well, Lucy, I will not ask too much of you. I dare say I am a romantic old fool; but if you do not dislike me, and if you do not love any one else, I see no reason why we should not make a very happy couple. Is it a bargain, Lucy?"

"Yes."

The baronet lifted her in his arms, and kissed her once upon the forehead; then, after quietly bidding her good night, he walked straight out of the house.

He walked straight out of the house, this

foolish old man, because there was some strong
emotion at work in his heart—neither joy, nor
triumph, but something almost akin to disappointment; some stifled and unsatisfied longing
which lay heavy and dull at his heart, as if he
had carried a corpse in his bosom. He carried
the corpse of that hope which had died at the
sound of Lucy's words. All the doubts and fears
and timid aspirations were ended now. He
must be contented, like other men of his age, to
be married for his fortune and his position.

Lucy Graham went slowly up the stairs to
her little room at the top of the house. She
placed her dim candle on the chest of drawers,
and seated herself on the edge of the white
bed; still and white as the draperies hanging
round her.

"No more dependence, no more drudgery, no
more humiliations," she said; "every trace of
the old life melted away—every clue to identity
buried and forgotten—except these, except these."

She had never taken her left hand from the
black ribbon at her throat. She drew it from

her bosom as she spoke, and looked at the object attached to it.

It was neither a locket, a miniature, nor a cross: it was a ring wrapped in an oblong piece of paper — the paper partly printed, partly written, yellow with age, and crumpled with much folding.

CHAPTER II.

ON BOARD THE ARGUS.

HE threw the end of his cigar into the water, and leaning his elbows upon the bulwarks, stared meditatively at the waves.

"How wearisome they are," he said; "blue, and green, and opal; opal, and blue, and green; all very well in their way, of course, but three months of them are rather too much, especially—"

He did not attempt to finish his sentence; his thoughts seemed to wander in the very midst o it, and carry him a thousand miles or so away.

"Poor little girl, how pleased she'll be!" he muttered, opening his cigar case, and lazily surveying its contents; "how pleased and how surprised! Poor little girl! After three years and a half, too; she *will* be surprised."

He was a young man of about five-and-twenty, with a dark face, bronzed by exposure to the

sun; he had handsome brown eyes, with a femi-
nine smile in them, that sparkled through his
black lashes, and a bushy beard and moustache
that covered the whole of the lower part of his
face.   He was tall, and powerfully built; he wore
a loose grey suit, and a felt hat, thrown carelessly
upon his black hair.   His name was George
Talboys, and he was aft-cabin passenger on board
the good ship Argus, laden with Australian wool,
and sailing from Sydney to Liverpool.

There were very few passengers in the aft-cabin
of the Argus.   An elderly wool-stapler, returning
to his native country with his wife and daughters,
after having made a fortune in the colonies; a
governess of five-and-thirty years of age going
home to marry a man to whom she had been
engaged fifteen years; the sentimental daughter of
a wealthy Australian wine merchant, invoiced to
England to finish her education, and George Talboys, were the only first-class passengers on board.

This George Talboys was the life and soul of
the vessel; nobody knew who or what he was, or
where he came from, but everybody liked him.

He sat at the bottom of the dinner table, and
assisted the captain in doing the honours of
the friendly meal.   He opened the champagne
bottles, and took wine with every one present;
he told funny stories, and led the laugh himself
with such a joyous peal, that the man must have
been a churl who could not have laughed for pure
sympathy.   He was a capital hand at speculation
and vingt-et-un, and all the merry round games,
which kept the little circle round the cabin lamp
so deep in innocent amusement, that a hurricane
might have howled overhead without their hearing
it; but he freely owned that he had no talent for
whist, and that he didn't know a knight from a
castle upon the chess-board.

Indeed, Mr. Talboys was by no means too
learned a gentleman. The pale governess had
tried to talk to him about fashionable literature,
but George had only pulled his beard, and stared
very hard at her, saying occasionally, " Ah, yes!"
and, " To be sure, ha!"

The sentimental young lady, going home to
finish her education, had tried him with Shelley

and Byron, and he had fairly laughed in her face, as if poetry were a joke. The wool-stapler sounded him upon politics, but he did not seem very deeply versed in them; so they let him go his own way, smoke his cigars and talk to the sailors, lounge over the bulwarks and stare at the water, and make himself agreeable to everybody in his own fashion. But when the Argus came to be within about a fortnight's sail of England everybody noticed a change in George Talboys. He grew restless and fidgety; sometimes so merry that the cabin rang with his laughter; sometimes moody and thoughtful. Favourite as he was amongst the sailors, they grew tired at last of answering his perpetual questions about the probable time of touching land. Would it be in ten days, in eleven, in twelve, in thirteen? Was the wind favourable? How many knots an hour was the vessel doing? Then a sudden passion would seize him, and he would stamp upon the deck, crying out that she was a rickety old craft, and that her owners were swindlers to advertise her as the fast-sailing Argus. She was not fit for passenger traffic; she was not fit to carry impatient living creatures, with hearts and souls; she was fit for nothing but to be laden with bales of stupid wool, that might rot on the sea and be none the worse for it.

The sun was dropping down behind the waves as George Talboys lighted his cigar upon this August evening. Only ten days more, the sailors had told him that afternoon, and they would see the English coast. " I will go ashore in the first boat that hails us," he cried; "I will go ashore in a cockle-shell. By Jove, if it comes to that, I will swim to land."

His friends in the aft-cabin, with the exception of the pale governess, laughed at his impatience: she sighed as she watched the young man, chafing at the slow hours, pushing away his untasted wine, flinging himself restlessly about upon the cabin sofa, rushing up and down the companion ladder, and staring at the waves.

As the red rim of the sun dropped into the water, the governess ascended the cabin-stairs for a stroll on deck, while the passengers sat over their wine below. She stopped when she came up to George, and standing by his side, watched the fading crimson in the western sky.

The lady was very quiet and reserved, seldom sharing in the after-cabin amusements, never laughing, and speaking very little; but she and George Talboys had been excellent friends throughout the passage.

"Does my cigar annoy you, Miss Morley?" he said, taking it out of his mouth.

"Not at all; pray do not leave off smoking. I only came up to look at the sunset. What a lovely evening!"

"Yes," yes, I dare say," he answered, impatiently; "yet so long, so long! Ten more interminable days and ten more weary nights before we land."

"Yes," said Miss Morley, sighing. "Do you wish the time shorter?"

"Do I?" cried George; "indeed I do. Don't you?"

"Scarcely.'

"But is there no one you love in England?

Is there no one you love looking out for your arrival?"

"I hope so," she said, gravely. They, were silent for some time, he smoking his cigar with a furious impatience, as if he could hasten the course of the vessel by his own restlessness; she looking out at the waning light with melancholy blue eyes: eyes that seemed to have faded with poring over closely-printed books and difficult needlework; eyes that had faded a little, perhaps, by reason of tears secretly shed in the dead hours of the lonely night.

"See!" said George, suddenly pointing in another direction from that towards which Miss Morley was looking, "there's the new moon."

She looked up at the pale crescent, her own face almost as pale and wan.

"This is the first time we have seen it. We must wish!" said George, "*I* know what *I* wish."

"What?"

"That we may get home quickly."

"My wish is that we may find no disappoin‧ment when we get there," said the governess, sadly.

" Disappointment !"

He started as if he had been struck, and asked what she meant by talking of disappointment.

"I mean this," she said, speaking rapidly, and with a restless motion of her thin hands; "I mean that as the end of this long voyage draws near, hope sinks in my heart: and a sick fear comes over me that at the last all may not be well. The person I go to meet may be changed in his feelings towards me; or he may retain all the old feeling until the moment of seeing me, and then lose it in a breath at sight of my poor wan face, for I was called a pretty girl, Mr. Talboys, when I sailed for Sydney, fifteen years ago; or he may be so changed by the world as to have grown selfish and mercenary, and he may welcome me for the sake of my fifteen years' savings. Again, he may be dead. He may have been well, perhaps, up to within a week of our landing, and in that last week may have taken a fever, and died an hour before our vessel anchors in the Mersey. I think of all these things, Mr. Talboys, and act the scenes over in my mind, and

feel the anguish of them twenty times a day.
Twenty times a day!" she repeated; "why, I do
it a thousand times a day."

George Talboys had stood motionless, with his
cigar in his hand, listening to her so intently that
as she said the last words, his hold relaxed, and
the cigar dropped into the water.

"I wonder," she continued, more to herself
than to him—"I wonder, looking back, to think
how hopeful I was when the vessel sailed; I never
thought then of disappointment, but I pictured
the joy of meeting, imagining the very words that
would be said, the very tones, the very looks; but
for this last month of the voyage, day by day,
and hour by hour, my heart sinks, and my hopeful fancies fade away, and I dread the end as
much as if I *knew* that I was going to England
to attend a funeral."

The young man suddenly changed his attitude,
and turned his face full upon his companion, with
a look of alarm. She saw in the pale light that
the colour had faded from his cheek.

"What a fool!" he cried, striking his clenched

fist upon the side of the vessel, " what a fool I am to be frightened at this ! Why do you come and say these things to me ? Why do you come and terrify me out of my senses, when I am going straight home to the woman I love; to a girl whose heart is as true as the light of heaven; and in whom I no more expect to find any change than I do to see another sun rise in to-morrow's sky ? Why do you come and try to put such fancies into my head, when I am going home to my darling wife ?"

" Your wife," she said; " that is different. There is no reason that my terrors should terrify you. I am going to England to rejoin a man to whom I was engaged to be married fifteen years ago. He was too poor to marry then, and when I was offered a situation as governess in a rich Australian family, I persuaded him to let me accept it, so that I might leave him free and unfettered to win his way in the world, while I saved a little money to help us when we began life together. I never meant to stay away so long, but things have gone badly with him in

England. That is my story, and you can understand my fears. They need not influence you.
Mine is an exceptional case."

"So is mine," said George, impatiently. "I
tell you that mine is an exceptional case, although
I swear to you that, until this moment, I have
never known a fear as to the result of my voyage
home. But you are right; your terrors have
nothing to do with me. You have been away
fifteen years; all kinds of things may happen in
fifteen years. Now, it is only three years and
a half this very month since I left England.
What can have happened in such a short time as
that?"

Miss Morley looked at him with a mournful
smile, but did not speak. His feverish ardour,
the freshness and impatience of his nature were
so strange and new to her, that she looked at him
half in admiration, half in pity.

"My pretty little wife! My gentle, innocent,
loving, little wife! Do you know, Miss Morley,"
he said, with all his old hopefulness of manner,
"that I left my little girl asleep, with her baby

in her arms, and with nothing but a few blotted lines to tell her why her faithful husband had deserted her ?"

" Deserted her ! " exclaimed the governess.

" Yes. I was a cornet in a cavalry regiment when I first met my little darling. We were quartered at a stupid sea-port town, where my pet lived with her shabby old father, a half-pay naval officer; a regular old humbug, as poor as Job, and with an eye for nothing but the main chance. I saw through all his shallow tricks to catch one of us for his pretty daughter. I saw all the pitiful, contemptible, palpable traps he set for big dragoons to walk into. I saw through his shabby-genteel dinners and public-house port; his fine talk of the grandeur of his family; his sham pride and independence, and the sham tears in his bleared old eyes when he talked of his only child. He was a drunken old hypocrite, and he was ready to sell my poor little girl to the highest bidder. Luckily for me, I happened just then to be the highest bidder; for my father is a rich man, Miss Morley, and as it was love

at first sight on both sides, my darling and I
made a match of it. No sooner, however, did
my father hear that I had married a penniless
little girl, the daughter of a tipsy old half-pay
lieutenant, than he wrote me a furious letter,
telling me he would never again hold any com-
munication with me, and that my yearly allowance would stop from my wedding-day. As there
was no remaining in such a regiment as mine,
with nothing but my pay to live on, and a pretty
little wife to keep, I sold out, thinking that before
the money that I got for my commission was
exhausted, I should be sure to drop into something. I took my darling to Italy, and we lived
there in splendid style as long as my two thousand pounds lasted; but when that began to
dwindle down to a couple of hundred or so, we
came back to England, and as my darling had a
fancy for being near that tiresome old father of
hers, we settled at the watering-place where he
lived. Well, as soon as the old man heard that
I had a couple of hundred pounds left, he expressed a wonderful degree of affection for us,

and insisted on our boarding in his house. We
consented, still to please my darling, who had just
then a peculiar right to have every whim and fancy
of her innocent heart indulged. We did board
with him, and finely he fleeced us; but when I
spoke of it to my little wife, she only shrugged her
shoulders, and said she did not like to be unkind
to 'poor papa.' So poor papa made away with
our little stock of money in no time; and as I
felt that it was now becoming necessary to look
about for something, I ran up to London, and
tried to get a situation as a clerk in a merchant's
office, or as accountant, or book-keeper, or something of that kind. But I suppose there was the
stamp of a heavy dragoon upon me, for do what
I would I couldn't get anybody to believe in my
capacity; and tired out, and down-hearted, I
returned to my darling, to find her nursing a
son and heir to his father's poverty. Poor little
girl, she was very low-spirited; and when I told
her that my London expedition had failed, she
fairly broke down, and burst into a storm of sobs
and lamentations, telling me that I ought not to

have married her if I could give her nothing but
poverty and misery; and that I had done her a
cruel wrong in making her my wife. By Heaven!
Miss Morley, her tears and reproaches drove me
almost mad; and I flew into a rage with her,
myself, her father, the world, and everybody in
it, and then ran out of the house, declaring that
I would never enter it again. I walked about
the streets all that day half out of my mind, and
with a strong inclination to throw myself into
the sea, so as to leave my poor girl free to make
a better match. 'If I drown myself, her father
must support her,' I thought; 'the old hypocrite
could never refuse her a shelter, but while I live
she has no claim on him.' I went down to a
rickety old wooden pier, meaning to wait there
till it was dark, and then drop quietly over the
end of it into the water; but while I sat there
smoking my pipe, and staring vacantly at the
sea-gulls, two men came down, and one of them
began to talk of the Australian gold-diggings,
and the great things that were to be done there.
It appeared that he was going to sail in a day or

two, and he was trying to persuade his companion
to join him in the expedition.

"I listened to these men for upwards of an
hour, following them up and down the pier with
my pipe in my mouth, and hearing all their talk.
After this I fell into conversation with them
myself, and ascertained that there was a vessel
going to leave Liverpool in three days, by which
vessel one of the men was going out. This man
gave me all the information I required, and told
me, moreover, that a stalwart young fellow such
as I was could hardly fail to do well in the
diggings. The thought flashed upon me so suddenly, that I grew hot and red in the face, and
trembled in every limb with excitement. This
was better than the water at any rate. Suppose
I stole away from my darling, leaving her safe
under her father's roof, and went and made a
fortune in the new world, and came back in a
twelvemonth to throw it into her lap; for I was
so sanguine in those days that I counted on
making my fortune in a year or so. I thanked
the man for his information, and late at night

strolled homewards. It was bitter winter weather, but I had been too full of passion to feel cold, and I walked through the quiet streets, with the snow drifting in my face, and a desperate hopefulness in my heart. The old man was sitting drinking brandy-and-water in his little dining-room; and my wife was upstairs, sleeping peacefully with the baby on her breast. I sat down and wrote a few brief lines, which told her that I never had loved her better than now when I seemed to desert her; that I was going to try my fortune in a new world; and that if I succeeded I should come back to bring her plenty and happiness, but that if I failed I should never look upon her face again. I divided the remainder of our money—something over forty pounds—into two equal portions, leaving one for her, and putting the other in my pocket. I knelt down and prayed for my wife and child, with my head upon the white counterpane that covered them. I wasn't much of a praying man at ordinary times, but God knows *that* was a heartfelt prayer. I kissed her once and the baby once, and then crept out of the room. The dining-room door was open, and the old man was nodding over his paper. He looked up as he heard my step in the passage, and asked me where I was going. 'To have a smoke in the street,' I answered; and as this was a common habit of mine, he believed me. Three nights after this I was out at sea, bound for Melbourne—a stecrage passenger, with a digger's tools for my baggage, and about seven shillings in my pocket."

"And you succeeded?" asked Miss Morley.

"Not till I had long despaired of success; not until poverty and I had become such old companions and bedfellows, that, looking back at my past life, I wondered whether that dashing, reckless, extravagant, luxurious, champagne-drinking dragoon could have really been the same man who sat on the damp ground gnawing a mouldy crust in the wilds of the new world. I clung to the memory of my darling, and the trust that I had in her love and truth, as the one keystone that kept the fabric of my past life together—the one star that lit the thick black darkness of the

future. I was hail fellow well met with bad men;
I was in the centre of riot, drunkenness, and
debauchery; but the purifying influence of my
love kept me safe from all. Thin and gaunt, the
half-starved shadow of what I once had been, I
saw myself one day in a broken bit of looking-
glass, and was frightened of my own face. But I
toiled on through all; through disappointment
and despair, rheumatism, fever, starvation, at the
very gates of death, I toiled on steadily to the
end; and in the end I conquered."

He was so brave in his energy and determination, in his proud triumph of success, and in
the knowledge of the difficulties he had van-
quished, that the pale governess could only look
at him in wondering admiration.

"How brave you were!" she said.

"Brave!" he cried, with a joyous peal of
laughter; "wasn't I working for my darling?
Through all the dreary time of that probation,
her pretty white hand beckoning me onwards to
a happy future? Why, I have seen her under
my wretched canvas tent, sitting by my side, with

her boy in her arms, as plainly as I had ever seen her in the one happy year of our wedded life. At last, one dreary, foggy morning, just three months ago; with a drizzling rain wetting me to the skin; up to my neck in clay and mire; half-starved; enfeebled by fever; stiff with rheumatism; a monster nugget turned up under my spade, and I came upon a gold deposit of some magnitude. A fortnight afterwards I was the richest man in all the little colony about me. I travelled post-haste to Sydney, realised my gold findings which were worth upwards of £20,000, and a fortnight afterwards took my passage for England in this vessel; and in ten days—in ten days I shall see my darling."

"But in all that time did you never write to your wife?"

"Never till a week before this vessel set sail. I could not write when everything looked so black. I could not write and tell her that I was fighting hard with despair and death. I waited for better fortune; and when that came, I wrote, telling her that I should be in England almost as

soon as my letter, and giving her an address
at a coffee-house in London, where she could
write to me, telling me where to find her;
though she is hardly likely to have left her
father's house."

He fell into a reverie after this, and puffed
meditatively at his cigar. His companion did not
disturb him. The last ray of the summer daylight
had died out, and the pale light of the crescent
moon only remained.

Presently George Talboys flung away his cigar,
and, turning to the governess, cried abruptly,
"Miss Morley, if, when I get to England, I hear
that anything has happened to my wife, I shall
fall down dead."

"My dear Mr. Talboys, why do you think
of these things? God is very good to us;
He will not afflict us beyond our power of en-
durance. I see all things, perhaps, in a melancholy light; for the long monotony of my life
has given me too much time to think over my
troubles."

"And my life has been all action, privation, toil, alternate hope and despair; I have had no time to think upon the chances of anything happening to my darling. What a blind, reckless fool I have been! Three years and a half, and not one line, one word from her, or from any mortal creature who knows her. Heaven above! what may not have happened?"

In the agitation of his mind he began to walk rapidly up and down the lonely deck, the governess following, and trying to soothe him.

"I swear to you, Miss Morley," he said, "that, till you spoke to me to-night, I never felt one shadow of fear; and now I have that sick, sinking dread at my heart, which you talked of an hour ago. Let me alone, please, to get over it my own way."

She drew silently away from him, and seated herself by the side of the vessel, looking over into the water.

CHAPTER III.

HIDDEN RELICS.

THE same August sun which had gone down
behind the waste of waters glimmered redly upon
the broad face of the old clock over that ivy-
covered archway which leads into the gardens of
Audley Court.

A fierce and crimson sunset. The mullioned
windows and the twinkling lattices are all ablaze
with the red glory; the fading light flickers upon
the leaves of the limes in the long avenue, and
changes the still fish-pond into a sheet of bur-
nished copper; even into those dim recesses of
briar and brushwood, amidst which the old well
is hidden, the crimson brightness penetrates
in fitful flashes, till the dank weeds and the
rusty iron wheel and broken woodwork seem as
if they were flecked with blood.

The lowing of a cow in the quiet meadows, the

splash of a trout in the fish-pond, the last notes
of a tired bird, the creaking of waggon-wheels
upon the distant road, every now and then breaking
the evening silence, only made the stillness of the
place seem more intense. It was almost oppressive, this twilight stillness. The very repose of
the place grew painful from its intensity, and
you felt as if a corpse must be lying somewhere
within that grey and ivy-covered pile of building—
so deathlike was the tranquillity of all around.

As the clock over the archway struck eight, a
door at the back of the house was softly opened,
and a girl came out into the gardens.

But even the presence of a human being
scarcely broke the silence; for the girl crept
slowly over the thick grass, and gliding into the
avenue by the side of the fish-pond, disappeared
under the rich shelter of the limes.

She was not, perhaps, positively a pretty girl;
but her appearance was of that order which is
commonly called interesting. Interesting, it may
be, because in the pale face and the light grey
eyes, the small features and compressed lips,

there was something which hinted at a power of
repression and self-control not common in a
woman of nineteen or twenty. She might have
been pretty, I think, but for the one fault in her
small oval face. This fault was an absence of
colour. Not one tinge of crimson flushed the
waxen whiteness of her cheeks; not one shadow
of brown redeemed the pale insipidity of her eyebrows and eyelashes; not one glimmer of gold or
auburn relieved the dull flaxen of her hair. Even
her dress was spoiled by this same deficiency;
the pale lavender muslin faded into a sickly grey,
and the ribbon knotted round her throat melted
into the same neutral hue.

Her figure was slim and fragile, and in spite of
her humble dress, she had something of the grace
and carriage of a gentlewoman ; but she was
only a simple country girl, called Phœbe Marks,
who had been nursemaid in Mr. Dawson's family,
and whom Lady Audley had chosen for her maid
after her marriage with Sir Michael.

Of course this was a wonderful piece of good
fortune for Phœbe, who found her wages trebled

and her work light in the well-ordered household at the Court; and who was therefore quite as much the object of envy amongst her particular friends as my lady herself in higher circles.

A man who was sitting on the broken woodwork of the well started as the lady's-maid came out of the dim shade of the limes and stood before him amongst the weeds and brushwood.

I have said before that this was a neglected spot: it lay in the midst of a low shrubbery, hidden away from the rest of the gardens, and only visible from the garret windows at the back of the west wing. "Why, Phœbe," said the man, shutting a clasp-knife with which he had been stripping the bark from a black-thorn stake, "you came upon me so still and sudden, that I thought you was an evil spirit. I've come across through the fields, and come in here at the gate agen the moat, and I was taking a rest before I came up to the house to ask if you was come back."

" I can see the well from my bed-room window, Luke," Phœbe answered, pointing to an open lattice in one of the gables. "I saw you sitting here, and came down to have a chat; it's better talking out here than in the house where there's always somebody listening."

The man was a big, broad-shouldered, stupid-looking clodhopper of about twenty-three years of age. His dark-red hair grew low upon his forehead, and his bushy brows met over a pair of greenish grey eyes; his nose was large and well shaped, but the mouth was coarse in form and animal in expression. Rosy-cheeked, red-haired, and bull-necked, he was not unlike one of the stout oxen grazing in the meadows round about the Court.

The girl seated herself lightly upon the wood-work at his side, and put one of her hands, which had grown white in her new and easy service, about his thick neck.

"Are you glad to see me, Luke?" she asked.

"Of course I'm glad, lass," he answered, boorishly, opening his knife again, and scraping away at the hedge-stake.

They were first cousins, and had been play-fellows in childhood, and sweethearts in early youth.

"You don't *seem* much as if you were glad," said the girl; "you might look at me, Luke, and tell me if you think my journey has improved me."

"It ain't put any colour into your cheeks, my girl," he said, glancing up at her from under his lowering eyebrows; "you're every bit as white as you was when you went away."

"But they say travelling makes people genteel, Luke. I've been on the Continent with my lady, through all manner of curious places; and you know when I was a child, Squire Horton's daughters taught me to speak a little French, and I found it so nice to be able to talk to the people abroad."

"Genteel!" cried Luke Marks, with a horse laugh; "who wants you to be genteel, I wonder? Not me for one; when you're my wife you won't have over-much time for gentility, my girl. French, too! Dang me, Phœbe, I suppose when we've saved money enough between us to buy a bit of a farm, you'll be *parlyvooing* to the cows?"

She bit her lip as her lover spoke, and looked away. He went on cutting and chopping at a rude handle he was fashioning to the stake, whistling softly to himself all the while, and not once looking at his cousin.

For some time they were silent; but by-and-by she said, with her face still turned away from her companion,—

"What a fine thing it is for Miss Graham, that was, to travel with her maid and her courier, and her chariot and four, and a husband that thinks there isn't one spot upon all the earth that's good enough for her to set her foot upon!"

"Ay, it is a fine thing, Phœbe, to have lots of money," answered Luke, "and I hope you'll be warned by that, my lass, to save up your wages agen we get married."

"Why, what was she in Mr. Dawson's house only three months ago?" continued the girl, as if she had not heard her cousin's speech. "What was she but a servant like me? Taking wages and working for them as hard, or harder than I did. You should have seen her shabby clothes,

Luke—worn and patched, and darned, and turned and twisted, yet always looking nice upon her, somehow. She gives me more as lady's-maid here than ever she got from Mr. Dawson then. Why, I've seen her come out of the parlour with a few sovereigns and a little silver in her hand, that master had just given her for her quarter's salary; and now look at her!"

"Never you mind her," said Luke; "take care of yourself, Phœbe; that's all you've got to do. What should you say to a public-house for you and me, by-and-by, my girl? There's a deal of money to be made out of a public-house."

The girl still sat with her face averted from her lover, her hands hanging listlessly in her lap, and her pale grey eyes fixed upon the last low streak of crimson dying out behind the trunks of the trees.

"You should see the inside of the house, Luke," she said; "it's a tumble-down looking place enough outside; but you should see my lady's rooms,—all pictures and gilding, and great looking-glasses that stretch from the ceiling to the floor.   Painted ceilings, too, that cost hundreds of pounds, the housekeeper told me, and all done for her."

"She's a lucky one," muttered Luke, with lazy indifference.

"You should have seen her while we were abroad, with a crowd of gentlemen always hanging about her; Sir Michael not jealous of them, only proud to see her so much admired.   You should have heard her laugh and talk with them; throwing all their compliments and fine speeches back at them, as it were, as if they had been pelting her with roses.   She set every body mad about her wherever she went.   Her singing, her playing, her painting, her dancing, her beautiful smile, and sunshiny ringlets!   She was always the talk of a place, as long as we stayed in it."

"Is she at home to-night?"

"No, she has gone out with Sir Michael to a dinner party, at the Beeches.   They've seven or eight miles to drive, and they won't be back till after eleven."

"Then I'll tell you what, Phœbe, if the inside

of the house is so mighty fine, I should like to have a look at it."

"You shall, then. Mrs. Barton, the house-keeper, knows you by sight, and she can't object to my showing you some of the best rooms."

It was almost dark when the cousins left the shrubbery and walked slowly to the house. The door by which they entered led into the servants' hall, on one side of which was the housekeeper's room. Phœbe Marks stopped for a moment to ask the housekeeper if she might take her cousin through some of the rooms, and having received permission to do so, lighted a candle at the lamp in the hall, and beckoned to Luke to follow her into the other part of the house.

The long, black oak corridors were dim in the ghostly twilight—the light carried by Phœbe looking only a poor speck of flame in the broad passages through which the girl led her cousin. Luke looked suspiciously over his shoulder now and then, half frightened of the creaking of his own hob-nailed boots.

"It's a mortal dull place, Phœbe," he said, as

they emerged from a passage into the principal
hall, which was not yet lighted; "I've heard
tell of a murder that was done here in old
times."

"There are murders enough in these times, as
to that, Luke," answered the girl, ascending the
staircase, followed by the young man.

She led the way through a great drawing-room,
rich in satin and ormolu, buhl and inlaid cabinets,
bronzes, cameos, statuettes, and trinkets, that
glistened in the dusky light; then through a
morning-room hung with proof engravings of
valuable pictures; through this into an ante-
chamber, where she stopped, holding the light
above her head.

The young man stared about him, open-mouthed
and open-eyed.

"It's a rare fine place," he said, "and must
have cost a power of money."

"Look at the pictures on the walls," said
Phœbe, glancing at the panels of the octagonal
chamber, which were hung with Claudes and
Poussins, Wouvermans and Cuyps, "I've heard

that those alone are worth a fortune. This is the entrance to my lady's apartments, Miss Graham that was." She lifted a heavy green cloth curtain which hung across a doorway, and led the astonished countryman into a fairy-like boudoir, and thence to a dressing-room, in which the open doors of a wardrobe and a heap of dresses flung about a sofa showed that it still remained exactly as its occupant had left it.

"I've all these things to put away before my lady comes home, Luke; you might sit down here while I do it, I shan't be long."

Her cousin looked round in gawky embarrassment, bewildered by the splendour of the room; and after some deliberation selected the most substantial of the chairs, on the extreme edge of which he carefully seated himself.

"I wish I could show you the jewels, Luke," said the girl; "but I can't, for she always keeps the keys herself; that's the case on the dressing-table there."

"What, *that?*" cried Luke, staring at the massive walnut-wood and brass inlaid casket.

"Why, that's big enough to hold every bit of clothes I've got ! "

"And it's as full as it can be of diamonds, rubies, pearls, and emeralds," answered Phœbe, busy as she spoke in folding the rustling silk dresses, and laying them one by one upon the shelves of the wardrobe. As she was shaking out the flounces of the last, a jingling sound caught her ear, and she put her hand into the pocket.

" I declare !" she exclaimed, " my lady has left her keys in her pocket for once in a way. I can show you the jewellery if you like, Luke."

"Well, I may as well have a look at it, my girl," he said, rising from his chair, and holding the light while his cousin unlocked the casket. He uttered a cry of wonder when he saw the ornaments glittering on white satin cushions. He wanted to handle the delicate jewels; to pull them about, and find out their mercantile value. Perhaps a pang of longing and envy shot through his heart as he thought how he would have liked to have taken one of them.

"Why, one of those diamond things would set us up in life, Phœbe," he said, turning a bracelet over and over in his big red hands.

"Put it down, Luke! Put it down directly!" cried the girl, with a look of terror; "how can you speak about such things?"

He laid the bracelet in its place with a reluctant sigh, and then continued his examination of the casket.

"What's this?" he asked presently, pointing to a brass knob in the framework of the box.

He pushed it as he spoke, and a secret drawer, lined with purple velvet, flew out of the casket.

"Look ye, here!" cried Luke, pleased at his discovery.

Phœbe Marks threw down the dress she had been folding, and went over to the toilette table.

"Why, I never saw this before," she said, "I wonder what there is in it?"

There was not much in it; neither gold nor gems; only a baby's little worsted shoe rolled up in a piece of paper, and a tiny lock of pale and

silky yellow hair, evidently taken from a baby's
head. Phœbe's grey eyes dilated as she examined
the little packet.

"So this is what my lady hides in the secret
drawer," she muttered.

"It's queer rubbish to keep in such a place,"
said Luke, carelessly.

The girl's thin lips curved into a curious smile.

"You will bear me witness where I found
this," she said, putting the little parcel into her
pocket.

"Why, Phœbe, you're never going to be such
a fool as to take that," cried the young man.

"I'd rather have this than the diamond
bracelet you would have liked to take," she
answered; "you shall have the public-house,
Luke."

CHAPTER IV.

IN THE FIRST PAGE OF THE "TIMES."

ROBERT AUDLEY was supposed to be a barrister. As a barrister was his name inscribed in the Law List; as a barrister, he had chambers in Fig-tree Court, Temple; as a barrister he had eaten the allotted number of dinners, which form the sublime ordeal through which the forensic aspirant wades on to fame and fortune. If these things can make a man a barrister, Robert Audley decidedly was one. But he had never either had a brief, or tried to get a brief, or even wished to have a brief in all those five years, during which his name had been painted upon one of the doors in Fig-tree Court. He was a handsome, lazy, care-for-nothing fellow, of about seven and-twenty; the only son of a younger brother of Sir Michael Audley. His father had left him £400 a year, which his friends had advised him to increase by being

called to the bar; and as he found it, after due
consideration, more trouble to oppose the wishes
of these friends, than to eat so many dinners, and
to take a set of chambers in the Temple; he
adopted the latter course, and unblushingly called
himself a barrister.

Sometimes, when the weather was very hot, and
he had exhausted himself with the exertion of
smoking his German pipe, and reading French
novels, he would stroll into the Temple Gardens,
and lying in some shady spot, pale and cool, with
his shirt collar turned down and a blue silk handkerchief tied loosely about his neck, would tell
grave benchers that he had knocked himself up
with over work.

The sly old benchers laughed at the pleasing
fiction; but they all agreed that Robert Audley
was a good fellow; a generous-hearted fellow;
rather a curious fellow too, with a fund of sly wit
and quiet humour, under his listless, dawdling,
indifferent, irresolute manner. A man who would
never get on in the world; but who would not
hurt a worm. Indeed, his chambers were con-

verted into a perfect dog-kennel by his habit of bringing home stray and benighted curs, who were attracted by his looks in the street, and followed him with abject fondness.

Robert always spent the hunting season at Audley Court; not that he was distinguished as a Nimrod, for he would quietly trot to covert upon a mild-tempered, stout-limbed, bay hack, and keep at a very respectful distance from the hard riders; his horse knowing quite as well as he did, that nothing was further from his thoughts than any desire to be in at the death.

The young man was a great favourite with his uncle, and by no means despised by his pretty, gipsy-faced, light-hearted, hoydenish cousin, Miss Alicia Audley. It might have seemed to other men that the partiality of a young lady, who was sole heiress to a very fine estate, was rather well worth cultivating, but it did not so occur to Robert Audley. Alicia was a very nice girl, he said, a jolly girl, with no nonsense about her—a girl of a thousand; but this was the highest point to which enthusiasm could carry him. The idea of turning

his cousin's girlish liking for him to some good
account never entered his idle brain. I doubt if
he even had any correct notion of the amount of
his uncle's fortune, and I am certain that he never
for one moment calculated upon the chances of
any part of that fortune ultimately coming to himself. So that when one fine spring morning,
about three months before the time of which I am
writing, the postman brought him the wedding
cards of Sir Michael and Lady Audley, together
with a very indignant letter from his cousin, setting
forth how her father had just married a wax-dol-
lish young person, no older than Alicia herself,
with flaxen ringlets and a perpetual giggle; for, I
am sorry to say, that Miss Audley's animus caused
her so to describe that pretty musical laugh which
had been so much admired in the late Miss Lucy
Graham—when, I say, these documents reached
Robert Audley—they elicited neither vexation nor
astonishment in the lymphatic nature of that gentleman. He read Alicia's angry, crossed and re-
crossed letter without so much as removing the
amber mouthpiece of his German pipe from his

moustachioed lips. When he had finished the
perusal of the epistle, which he read with his dark
eyebrows elevated to the centre of his forehead
(his only manner of expressing surprise, by the
way), he deliberately threw that and the wedding
cards into the waste-paper basket, and putting
down his pipe, prepared himself for the exertion
of thinking out the subject.

"I always said the old buffer would marry,"
he muttered, after about half an hour's reverie.
" Alicia and my lady, the step-mother, will go at
it hammer and tongs. I hope they won't quarrel
in the hunting season, or say unpleasant things to
each other at the dinner-table : rows always upset
a man's digestion."

At about twelve o'clock on the morning following that night upon which the events recorded in
my last chapter had taken place, the Baronet's
nephew strolled out of the Temple, Blackfriars-
ward, on his way to the City. He had in an evil
hour obliged some necessitous friend by putting
the ancient name of Audley across a bill of accom-
modation, which bill not having been met by the

drawer, Robert was called upon to pay. For this purpose he sauntered up Ludgate Hill, with his blue necktie fluttering in the hot August air, and thence to a refreshingly cool banking-house in a shady court out of St. Paul's Churchyard, where he made arrangements for selling out a couple of hundred pounds worth of consols.

He had transacted this business, and was loitering at the corner of the court, waiting for a chance Hansom, to convey him back to the Temple, when he was almost knocked down by a man of about his own age, who dashed headlong into the narrow opening.

"Be so good as to look where you're going, my friend!" Robert remonstrated, mildly, to the impetuous passenger; "you might give a man warning before you throw him down and trample upon him."

The stranger stopped suddenly, looked very hard at the speaker, and then gasped for breath.

"Bob!" he cried, in a tone expressive of the most intense astonishment; "I only touched

British ground after dark last night, and to think
that I should meet you this morning ! "

"I've seen you somewhere before, my bearded
friend," said Mr. Audley, calmly scrutinising the
animated face of the other, " but I'll be hanged if
I can remember when or where."

"What ! " exclaimed the stranger, reproachfully, "you don't mean to say that you've forgotten George Talboys ?"

" *No, I have not !* " said Robert, with an em-
phasis by no means usual to him ; and then
hooking his arm into that of his friend, he led
him into the shady court, saying with his old
indifference, " and now, George, tell us all about
it."

George Talboys did tell him all about it.   He
told that very story which he had related ten
days before to the pale governess on board the
Argus; and then, hot and breathless, he said that
he had a bundle of Australian notes in his pocket,
and that he wanted to bank them at Messrs. ——,
who had been his bankers many years before.

"If you'll believe me, I've only just left their

counting-house," said Robert. "I'll go back with you, and we'll settle that matter in five minutes."

They did contrive to settle it in about a quarter of an hour; and then Robert Audley was for starting off immediately for the Crown and Sceptre, or the Castle, Richmond, where they could have a bit of dinner, and talk over those good old times when they were together at Eton. But George told his friend that before he went anywhere, before he shaved, or broke his fast, or in any way refreshed himself after a night journey from Liverpool by express train, he must call at a certain coffee-house in Bridge Street, Westminster, where he expected to find a letter from his wife.

"Then I'll go there with you," said Robert. "The idea of your having a wife, George; what a preposterous joke."

As they dashed through Ludgate Hill, Fleet Street and the Strand in a fast Hansom, George Talboys poured into his friend's ear all those wild hopes and dreams which had usurped such a dominion over his sanguine nature.

"I shall take a villa on the banks of the Thames, Bob," he said, "for the little wife and myself; and we'll have a yacht, Bob, old boy, and you shall lie on the deck and smoke while my pretty one plays her guitar and sings songs to us. She's for all the world like one of those what's-its-names, who got poor old Ulysses into trouble," added the young man, whose classic lore was not very great.

The waiters at the Westminster coffee-house stared at the hollow-eyed, unshaven stranger, with his clothes of colonial cut, and his boisterous, excited manner; but he had been an old frequenter of the place in his military days, and when they heard who he was they flew to do his bidding.

He did not want much—only a bottle of soda water, and to know if there was a letter at the bar directed to George Talboys.

The waiter brought the soda water before the young men had seated themselves in a shady box near the disused fireplace. No; there was no letter for that name.

The waiter said it with consummate indifference, while he mechanically dusted the little mahogany table.

George's face blanched to a deadly whiteness.

"Talboys," he said; "perhaps you didn't hear the name distinctly—T, A, L, B, O, Y, S. Go and look again; there *must* be a letter."

The waiter shrugged his shoulders as he left the room, and returned in three minutes to say that there was no name at all resembling Talboys in the letter rack. There was Brown, and Saunderson, and Pinchbeck; only three letters altogether.

The young man drank his soda water in silence, and then leaning his elbows upon the table, covered his face with his hands. There was something in his manner which told Robert Audley that this disappointment, trifling as it might appear, was in reality a very bitter one. He seated himself opposite to his friend, but did not attempt to address him.

By-and-by George looked up, and mechanically taking a greasy *Times* newspaper of the day before from a heap of journals on the table, stared vacantly at the first page.

I cannot tell how long he sat blankly staring at one paragraph amongst the list of deaths, before his dazed brain took in its full meaning; but after a considerable pause he pushed the newspaper over to Robert Audley, and with a face that had changed from its dark bronze to a sickly, chalky, greyish white, and with an awful calmness in his manner, he pointed with his finger to a line which ran thus :—

"On the 24th inst., at Ventnor, Isle of Wight, Helen Talboys, aged twenty-two."

CHAPTER V.

THE HEADSTONE AT VENTNOR.

YES: there it was, in black and white—"Helen Talboys, aged twenty-two."

When George told the governess on board the Argus that if he heard any evil tidings of his wife he should drop down dead, he spoke in perfect good faith; and yet here were the worst tidings that could come to him, and he sat rigid, white, and helpless, staring stupidly at the shocked face of his friend.

The suddenness of the blow had stunned him. In his strange and bewildered state of mind he began to wonder what had happened, and why it was that one line in the *Times* newspaper could have so horrible an effect upon him.

Then by degrees even this vague consciousness of his misfortune faded slowly out of his mind, succeeded by a painful consciousness of external things.

The hot August sunshine; the dusty window panes and shabby painted blinds; a file of fly-blown play-bills fastened to the wall; the blank and empty fire-place; a bald-headed old man nodding over the *Morning Advertiser;* the slip-shod waiter folding a tumbled table-cloth, and Robert Audley's handsome face looking at him full of compassionate alarm. He knew that all these things took gigantic proportions, and then, one by one, melted into dark blots that swam before his eyes. He knew that there was a great noise as of half-a-dozen furious steam-engines tearing and grinding in his ears, and he knew nothing more, except that somebody or something fell heavily to the ground.

He opened his eyes upon the dusky evening in a cool and shaded room, the silence only broken by the rumbling of wheels at a distance.

He looked about him wonderingly, but half indifferently. His old friend, Robert Audley, was seated by his side smoking. George was lying on a low iron bedstead opposite to an open window, in which there was a stand of flowers and two or three birds in cages.

"You don't mind the pipe, do you, George?" his friend asked quietly.

"No."

He lay for some time looking at the flowers and the birds: one canary was singing a shrill hymn to the setting sun.

"Do the birds annoy you, George? Shall I take them out of the room?"

"No: I like to hear them sing."

Robert Audley knocked the ashes out of his pipe, laid the precious meerschaum tenderly upon the mantel-piece, and going into the next room, returned presently with a cup of strong tea.

"Take this, George," he said, as he placed the cup on a little table close to George's pillow; "it will do your head good."

The young man did not answer, but looked slowly round the room, and then at his friend's grave face.

"Bob," he said, "where are we?"

" In my chambers, my dear boy, in the Temple. You have no lodgings of your own, so you may as well stay with me while you're in town."

George passed his hand once or twice across his forehead, and then, in a hesitating manner, said quietly—

" That neswspaper this morning, Bob; what was it ? "

" Never mind just now, old boy; drink some tea.'

" Yes, yes," cried George, impatiently, raising himself upon the bed, and staring about him with hollow eyes, " I remember all about it. Helen, my Helen! my wife, my darling, my only love ! Dead ! dead ! "

" George," said Robert Audley, laying his hand gently upon the young man's arm, " you must remember that the person whose name you saw in the paper may not be your wife. There may have been some other Helen Talboys."

" No, no," he cried, " the age corresponds with hers, and Talboys is such an uncommon name."

"It may be a misprint for Talbot."

"No, no, no; my wife is dead!"

He shook off Robert's restraining hand, and rising from the bed, walked straight to the door.

"Where are you going?" exclaimed his friend.

"To Ventnor, to see her grave."

"Not to-night, George, not to-night. I will go with you myself by the first train to-morrow."

Robert led him back to the bed, and gently forced him to lie down again. He then gave him an opiate which had been left for him by the medical man whom they had called in at the coffee-house in Bridge Street, when George fainted.

So George Talboys fell into a heavy slumber, and dreamed that he went to Ventnor, to find his wife alive and happy, but wrinkled, old, and grey, and to find his son grown into a young man.

Early the next morning he was seated opposite to Robert Audley in the first-class carriage of an express, whirling through the pretty open country towards Portsmouth.

They rode from Ryde to Ventnor under the burning heat of the mid-day sun. As the two young men alighted from the coach, the people standing about stared at George's white face and untrimmed beard.

"What are we to do, George?" Robert Audley asked. "We have no clue to finding the people you want to see."

The young man looked at him with a pitiful, bewildered expression. The big dragoon was as helpless as a baby; and Robert Audley, the most vacillating and unenergetic of men, found himself called upon to act for another. He rose superior to himself and equal to the occasion.

"Had we better ask at one of the hotels about a Mrs. Talboys, George?" he said.

"Her father's name was Maldon," George muttered; "he could never have sent her here to die alone."

They said nothing more, but Robert walked straight to an hotel, where he inquired for a Mr. Maldon.

"Yes," they told him, "there was a gentleman of that name stopping at Ventnor, a Captain Maldon; his daughter was lately dead. The waiter would go and inquire for the address."

The hotel was a busy place at this season; people hurrying in and out, and a great bustle of grooms and waiters about the hall.

George Talboys leaned against the door-post with much the same look in his face as that which had frightened his friend in the Westminster coffee-house.

The worst was confirmed *now*. His wife, Captain Maldon's daughter, was dead.

The waiter returned in about five minutes to say that Captain Maldon was lodging at Lansdowne Cottages, No. 4.

They easily found the house, a shabby bow-windowed cottage, looking towards the water.

Was Captain Maldon at home? No, the landlady said; he had gone out to the beach with his little grandson. Would the gentlemen walk in and sit down a bit?

George mechanically followed his friend into

the little front parlour—dusty, shabbily furnished,
and disorderly, with a child's broken toys scattered
on the floor, and the scent of stale tobacco hanging about the muslin window curtains.

"Look!" said George, pointing to a picture
over the mantel-piece.

It was his own portrait, painted in the old
dragooning days. A pretty good likeness, repre-
senting him in uniform, with his charger in the
background.

Perhaps the most animated of men would
have been scarcely so wise a comforter as Robert
Audley. He did not utter a word to the stricken
widower, but quietly seated himself with his
back to George, looking out of the open
window.

For some time the young man wandered restlessly about the room, looking at and sometimes
touching the knicknacks lying here and there.

Her work-box, with an unfinished piece of
work; her album, full of extracts from Byron
and Moore, written in his own scrawling hand;
some books which he had given her, and a bunch

of withered flowers in a vase they had bought in
Italy.

"Her portrait used to hang by the side of
mine," he muttered; "I wonder what they have
done with it?" .

By-and-by he said, after about half-an-hour's
silence—

"I should like to see the woman of the house;
I should like to ask her about ——"

He broke down, and buried his face in his
hands.

Robert summoned the landlady. She was a
goodnatured, garrulous creature, used to sickness and death, for many of her lodgers came
to her to die. She told all the particulars of
Mrs. Talboys' last hours; how she had come to
Ventnor only a week before her death in the last
stage of decline; and how day by day she had
gradually but surely sunk under the fatal malady.
"Was the gentleman any relative?" she asked
of Robert Audley, as George sobbed aloud.

"Yes, he is the lady's husband."

"What!" the woman cried; "him as deserted

her so cruel, and left her with her pretty boy upon her poor old father's hands, which Captain Maldon has told me often, with the tears in his poor eyes?"

"I did not desert her," George cried out; and then he told the history of his three years' struggle.

"Did she speak of me?" he asked; "did she speak of me at—at—the last?"

"No, she went off as quiet as a lamb. She said very little from the first; but the last day she knew nobody, not even her little boy nor her poor old father, who took on awful. Once she went off wild like, talking about her mother, and about the cruel shame it was to have to die in a strange place, till it was quite pitiful to hear her."

"Her mother died when she was quite a child," said George. "To think that she should remember her and speak of her, but never once of me."

The woman took him into the little bed-room in which his wife had died. He knelt down by

o 2

the bed and kissed the pillow tenderly, the landlady crying as he did so.

While he was kneeling, praying perhaps, with his face buried in this humble snow-white pillow, the woman took something from a drawer. She gave it to him when he rose from his knees; it was a long tress of hair wrapped in silver paper.

"I cut this off when she lay in her coffin," she said, "poor dear!"

He pressed the soft lock to his lips. "Yes," he murmured; "this is the dear hair that I have kissed so often when her head lay upon my shoulder. But it always had a rippling wave in it then, and now it seems smooth and straight."

"It changes in illness," said the landlady. "If you'd like to see where they have laid her, Mr. Talboys, my little boy shall show you the way to the churchyard."

So George Talboys and his faithful friend walked to the quiet spot, where beneath a mound of earth, to which the patches of fresh turf hardly adhered, lay that wife of whose welcoming smile George had dreamed so often in the far antipodes.

Robert left the young man by the side of this new-made grave, and returning in about a quarter of an hour, found that he had not once stirred.

He looked up presently, and said that if there was a stonemason's anywhere near he should like to give an order.

They very easily found the stonemason, and sitting down amidst the fragmentary litter of the man's yard, George Talboys wrote in pencil this brief inscription for the headstone of his dead wife's grave:—

Sacred to the Memory of

HELEN,

THE BELOVED WIFE OF GEORGE TALBOYS,

Who departed this life

August 24th, 1857, aged 22,

Deeply regretted by her sorrowing Husband.

CHAPTER VI.

ANYWHERE, ANYWHERE OUT OF THE WORLD.

WHEN they returned to Landsdowne Cottage
they found the old man had not yet come in, so
they walked down to the beach to look for him.
After a brief search they found him, sitting upon
a heap of pebbles, reading a newspaper and
eating filberts. The little boy was at some distance from his grandfather, digging in the sand
with a wooden spade. The crape round the old
man's shabby hat, and the child's poor little black
frock, went to George's heart. Go where he
would he met confirmation of this great grief of
his life. His wife was dead.

"Mr. Maldon," he said, as he approached his
father-in-law.

The old man looked up, and, dropping his newspaper, rose from the pebbles with a ceremonious
bow. His faded, light hair was tinged with grey;

he had a pinched hook nose, watery blue eyes, and an irresolute-looking mouth; he wore his shabby dress with an affectation of foppish gentility; an eye-glass dangled over his closely-buttoned-up waistcoat, and he carried a cane in his ungloved hand.

"Good heavens!" cried George, "don't you know me?"

Mr. Maldon started and coloured violently, with something of a frightened look, as he recognised his son-in-law.

"My dear boy," he said, "I did not; for the first moment I did not; that beard makes such a difference. You find the beard makes a great difference, do you not, sir?" he said, appealing to Robert.

"Great Heaven!" exclaimed George Talboys, "is this the way you welcome me? I come to England to find my wife dead within a week of my touching land, and you begin to chatter to me about my beard,—you, her father!"

"True! true!" muttered the old man, wiping his blood-shot eyes; "a sad shock, a sad shock, my dear George. If you'd only been here a week earlier?"

"If I had," cried George, in an outburst of grief and passion, "I scarcely think that I would have *let* her die. I would have disputed for her with death. I would! I would! O God! why did not the Argus go down with every soul on board her before I came to see this day?"

He began to walk up and down the beach, his father-in-law looking helplessly at him, rubbing his feeble eyes with a handkerchief.

"I've a strong notion that that old man didn't treat his daughter too well," thought Robert, as he watched the half-pay lieutenant. "He seems, for some reason or other, to be half afraid of George."

While the agitated young man walked up and down in a fever of regret and despair, the child ran to his grandfather and clung about the tails of his coat.

"Come home, grandpa', come home," he said. "I'm tired."

George Talboys turned at the sound of the

babyish voice, and long and earnestly looked at the boy.

He had his father's brown eyes and dark hair.

"My darling! my darling!" said George, taking the child in his arms, "I am your father, come across the sea to find you. Will you love me?"

The little fellow pushed him away. "I don't know you," he said. "I love grandpa' and Mrs. Monks, at Southampton."

"Georgey has a temper of his own, sir," said the old man. "He has been spoiled."

They walked slowly back to the cottage, and once more George Talboys told the history of that desertion which had seemed so cruel. He told, too, of the twenty thousand pounds banked by him the day before. He had not the heart to ask any questions about the past, and his father-in-law only told him that a few months after his departure they had gone from the place where George left them to live at Southampton, where Helen got a few pupils for the piano, and where they managed pretty well till her health failed, and she fell into the decline of which she died. Like most sad stories, it was a very brief one.

"The boy seems fond of you, Mr. Maldon," said George, after a pause.

"Yes, yes," answered the old man, smoothing the child's curling hair, "yes, Georgey is very fond of his grandfather."

"Then he had better stop with you. The interest of my money will be about six hundred a year. You can draw a hundred of that for Georgey's education, leaving the rest to accumulate till he is of age. My friend here will be trustee, and if he will undertake the charge, 1 will appoint him guardian to the boy, allowing him for the present to remain under your care."

"But why not take care of him yourself, George?" asked Robert Audley.

"Because I shall sail in the very next vessel that leaves Liverpool for Australia. I shall be better in the diggings or the backwoods than ever I could be here. I'm broken for a civilised life from this hour, Bob."

The old man's weak eyes sparkled as George declared this determination.

"My poor boy, I think you're right," he said, "I really think you're right. The change, the wild life, the—the——" He hesitated and broke down, as Robert looked earnestly at him.

"You're in a great hurry to get rid of you're son-in-law, I think, Mr. Maldon," he said gravely.

"Get rid of him, dear boy! Oh, no, no! But for his own sake, my dear sir, for his own sake, you know."

"I think for his own sake he'd much better stay in England and look after his son," said Robert.

"But I tell you I can't," cried George; "every inch of this accursed ground is hateful to me—I want to run out of it as I would out of a graveyard. I'll go back to town to-night, get that business about the money settled early to-morrow morning, and start for Liverpool without a moment's delay. I shall be better when I've put half the world between me and her grave."

Before he left the house he stole out to the

landlady, and asked some more questions about his dead wife.

"Were they poor?" he asked; "were they pinched for money while she was ill?"

"Oh, no!" the woman answered; "though the captain dresses shabby, he has always plenty of sovereigns in his purse. The poor lady wanted for nothing."

George was relieved at this, though it puzzled him to know where the drunken half-pay lieutenant could have contrived to find money for all the expenses of his daughter's illness.

But he was too thoroughly broken down by the calamity which had befallen him to be able to think much of anything, so he asked no further questions, but walked with his father-in-law and Robert Audley down to the boat by which they were to cross to Portsmouth.

The old man bade Robert a very ceremonious adieu.

"You did not introduce me to your friend, by-the-bye, my dear boy," he said. George stared at him, muttered something indistinct, and ran down the ladder to the boat before Mr. Maldon could repeat his request. The steamer sped away through the sunset, and the outlines of the island melted in the horizon as they neared the opposite shore.

"To think," said George, "that two nights ago at this time I was steaming into Liverpool, full of the hope of clasping her to my heart, and to-night I am going away from her grave!"

The document which appointed Robert Audley as guardian to little George Talboys was drawn up in a solicitor's office the next morning.

"It's a great responsibility," exclaimed Robert; "I, guardian to anybody or anything! I, who never in my life could take care of myself!"

"I trust in your noble heart, Bob," said George, "I know you will take care of my poor orphan boy, and see that he is well used by his grandfather. I shall only draw enough from George's fortune to take me back to Sydney, and then begin my old work again."

But it seemed as if George was destined to be himself the guardian of his son; for when he reached Liverpool, he found that a vessel had just sailed, and that there would not be another for a month; so he returned to London, and once more threw himself upon Robert Audley's hospitality.

The barrister received him with open arms; he gave him the room with the birds and flowers, and had a bed put up in his dressing-room for himself. Grief is so selfish that George did not know the sacrifices his friend made for his comfort. He only knew that for him the sun was darkened, and the business of life done. He sat all day long smoking cigars, and staring at the flowers and canaries, chafing for the time to pass that he might be far out at sea.

But, just as the hour was drawing near for the sailing of the vessel, Robert Audley came in one day full of a great scheme. A friend of his, another of those barristers whose last thought is of a brief, was going to St. Petersburg to spend the winter, and wanted Robert to accompany him. Robert would only go on condition that George went too.

For a long time the young man resisted, but when he found that Robert was, in a quiet way, thoroughly determined upon not going without him, he gave in, and consented to join the qarty. "What did it matter?" he said. "One place was the same to him as another, anywhere out of England; what did he care where?"

This was not a very cheerful way of looking at things, but Robert Audley was quite satisfied with having won his consent.

The three young men started under very favourable circumstances, carrying letters of introduction to the most influential inhabitants of the Russian capital.

Before leaving England Robert wrote to his cousin Alicia, telling her of his intended departure with his old friend George Talboys, whom he had lately met for the first time after a lapse of years, and who had just lost his wife.

Alicia's reply came by return of post, and ran thus :—

"MY DEAR ROBERT,—How cruel of you to

run away to that horrid St. Petersburg before the hunting season! I have heard that people lose their noses in that disagreeable climate, and as yours is rather a long one, I should advise you to return before the very severe weather sets in. What sort of person is this young Mr. Talboys? If he is very agreeable you may bring him to the Court as soon as you return from your travel. Lady Audley tells me to request you to secure her a set of sables. You are not to consider the price, but to be sure that they are the handsomest that can be obtained. Papa is perfectly absurd about his new wife, and she and I cannot get on together at all; not that she is disagreeable to me, for, as far as that goes, she makes herself agreeable to every one; but she is so irretrievably childish and silly.

"Believe me to be, my dear Robert,

"Your affectionate Cousin,

"ALICIA AUDLEY."

CHAPTER VII.

AFTER A YEAR.

THE first year of George Talboys' widowhood passed away; the deep band of crape about his hat grew brown and rusty, and as the last burning day of another August faded out, he sat smoking cigars in the quiet chambers in Fig Tree Court, much as he had done the year before, when the horror of his grief was new to him, and every object in life, however trifling or however important, seemed saturated with his one great sorrow.

But the big ex-dragoon had survived his affliction by a twelvemonth, and hard as it may be to have to tell it, he did not look much the worse for it. Heaven knows what inner change may have been worked by that bitter disappointment! Heaven knows what wasted agonies of remorse and self-reproach may not have racked

George's honest heart as he lay awake at nights thinking of the wife he had abandoned in the pursuit of a fortune which she never lived to share.

Once, while they were abroad, Robert Audley ventured to congratulate him upon his recovered spirits. He burst into a bitter laugh.

"Do you know, Bob," he said, "that when some of our fellows were wounded in India, they came home bringing bullets inside them. They did not talk of them, and they were stout and hearty, and looked as well, perhaps, as you or I; but every change in the weather, however slight, every variation of the atmosphere, however trifling, brought back the old agony of their wounds as sharp as ever they had felt it on the battle-field. I've had my wound, Bob; I carry the bullet still, and I shall carry it into my coffin."

The travellers returned from St. Petersburg in the spring, and George again took up his quarters in his old friend's chambers, only leaving them now and then to run down to South-

ampton and take a look at his little boy. He
always went loaded with toys and sweetmeats to
give to the child; but, for all this, Georgey
would not become very familiar with his papa,
and the young man's heart sickened as he began
to fancy that even his child was lost to him.

"What can I do?" he thought. "If I take
him away from his grandfather I shall break his
heart; if I let him remain he will grow up a
stranger to me, and care more for that drunken
old hypocrite than for his own father. But then
what could an ignorant heavy dragoon like me do
with such a child? What could I teach him
except to smoke cigars, and idle about all day
with his hands in his pockets?"

So the anniversary of that 30th of August,
upon which George had seen the advertisement of
his wife's death in the *Times* newspaper, came
round for the first time, and the young man put
off his black clothes and the shabby crape from
his hat, and laid his mourning garments in a
trunk in which he kept a packet of his wife's
letters, and that lock of hair which had been cut

from her head after death. Robert Audley had
never seen either the letters or the long tress of
silky hair; nor, indeed, had George ever mentioned the name of his dead wife after that one
day at Ventnor on which he learned the full particulars of her decease.

"I shall write to my cousin Alicia to-day,
George," the young barrister said, upon this very
30th of August. "Do you know that the day
after to-morrow is the 1st of September? I shall
write and tell her that we will both run down to
the Court for a week's shooting."

"No, no, Bob: go by yourself; they don't
want me, and I'd rather——"

"Bury yourself in Fig Tree Court, with no
company but my dogs and canaries! No,
George, you shall do nothing of the kind."

"But I don't care for shooting."

"And do you suppose I care for it?" cried
Robert, with charming naïveté. "Why, man, I
don't know a partridge from a pigeon, and it
might be the 1st of April instead of the 1st of
September for aught I care. I never hit a bird

in my life, but I have hurt my own shoulder
with the weight of my gun. I only go down to
Essex for the change of air, the good dinners,
and the sight of my uncle's honest, handsome
face. Besides, this time I've another induce-
ment, as I want to see this fair-haired paragon,
my new aunt. You'll go with me, George?"

"Yes, if you really wish it."

The quiet form which his grief had taken after
its first brief violence left him as submissive as a
child to the will of his friend; ready to go anywhere or do anything; never enjoying himself,
or originating any enjoyment, but joining in the
pleasures of others with a hopeless, quiet, un-
complaining, unobtrusive resignation peculiar to
his simple nature. But the return of post
brought a letter from Alicia Audley, to say that
the two young men could not be received at the
Court.

" There are seventeen spare bed-rooms," wrote
the young lady, in an indignant running hand,
" but for all that, my dear Robert, you can't come:
for my lady has taken it into her silly head that

she is too ill to entertain visitors (there is no more
the matter with her than there is with me), and
she cannot have gentlemen (great rough men, she
says) in the house. Please apologise to your
friend Mr. Talboys, and tell him that papa hopes
to see you both in the hunting season."

"My lady's airs and graces shan't keep us out
of Essex for all that," said Robert, as he twisted
the letter into a pipe-light for his big meerschaum. "I'll tell you what we'll do, George;
there's a glorious inn at Audley, and plenty of
fishing in the neighbourhood : we'll go there and
have a week's sport. Fishing is much better than
shooting; you've only to lie on a bank and stare
at your line; I don't find that you often catch
anything, but it's very pleasant."

He held the twisted letter to the feeble spark
of fire glimmering in the grate as he spoke, and
then changing his mind, deliberately unfolded it
and smoothed the crumpled paper with his hand.

"Poor little Alicia!" he said thoughtfully;
"it's rather hard to treat her letters so cavalierly
—I'll keep it;" upon which Mr. Robert Audley

put the note back into its envelope, and afterwards thrust it into a pigeon-hole in his office
desk marked *important.* Heaven knows what
wonderful documents there were in this particular
pigeon-hole, but I do not think it likely to have
contained anything of great judicial value. If
any one could at that moment have told the
young barrister that so simple a thing as his
cousin's brief letter would one day come to be a
link in that terrible chain of evidence afterwards
to be slowly forged in the one only criminal case
in which he was ever to be concerned, perhaps
Mr. Robert Audley would have lifted his eyebrows
a little higher than usual.

So the two young men left London the next
day with one portmanteau and a rod and tackle
between them, and reached the straggling, old-
fashioned, fast decaying village of Audley in time
to order a good dinner at the Sun Inn.

Audley Court was about three-quarters of a
mile from the village, lying, as I have said, deep
down in a hollow, shut in by luxuriant timber.
You could only reach it by a cross road, bor-

dered by trees, and as trimly kept as the avenues
in a gentleman's park. It was a dreary place
enough, even in all its rustic beauty, for so bright
a creature as the late Miss Lucy Graham, but the
generous baronet had transformed the interior of
the grey old mansion into a little palace for his
young wife, and Lady Audley seemed as happy as
a child surrounded by new and costly toys.

In her better fortunes, as in her old days of
dependence, wherever she went she seemed to
take sunshine and gladness with her. In spite of
Miss Alicia's undisguised contempt for her step-
mother's childishness and frivolity, Lucy was
better loved and more admired than the baronet's
daughter. That very childishness had a charm
which few could resist. The innocence and candour of an infant beamed in Lady Audley's fair
face, and shone out of her large and liquid blue
eyes. The rosy lips, the delicate nose, the pro-
fusion of fair ringlets, all contributed to preserve
to her beauty the character of extreme youth and
freshness. She owned to twenty years of age,
but it was hard to believe her more than seven-

teen. Her fragile figure, which she loved to
dress in heavy velvets and stiff rustling silks,
till she looked like a child tricked out for a mas-
querade, was as girlish as if she had but just left
the nursery. All her amusements were childish.
She hated reading, or study of any kind, and
loved society; rather than be alone she would
admit Phœbe Marks into her confidence, and loll
on one of the sofas in her luxurious dressing-
room, discussing a new costume for some coming
dinner party, or sit chattering to the girl, with
her jewel box beside her, upon the satin cushions,
and Sir Michael's presents spread out in her lap,
while she counted and admired her treasures.

She had appeared at several public balls at
Chelmsford and Colchester, and was immediately
established as the belle of the county. Pleased
with her high position and her handsome house;
with every caprice gratified, every whim indulged;
admired and caressed wherever she went; fond of
her generous husband; rich in a noble allowance
of pin-money; with no poor relations to worry
her with claims upon her purse or patronage, it

would have been hard to find in the county of Essex a more fortunate creature than Lucy, Lady Audley.

The two young men loitered over the dinner-table in the private sitting-room at the Sun Inn. The windows were thrown wide open, and the fresh country air blew in upon them as they dined. The weather was lovely; the foliage of the woods touched here and there with faint gleams of the earliest tints of autumn; the yellow corn still standing in some of the fields, in others just falling under the shining sickle; while in the narrow lanes you met great waggons drawn by broad-chested cart horses, carrying home the rich golden store. To any one who has been, during the hot summer months, pent up in London, there is in the first taste of rustic life a kind of sensuous rapture scarcely to be described. George Talboys felt this, and in this he experienced the nearest approach to enjoyment that he had ever known since his wife's death.

The clock struck five as they finished dinner.

"Put on your hat, George," said Robert Audley;

"they don't dine at the Court till seven; we shall have time to stroll down and see the old place and its inhabitants."

The landlord, who had come into the room with a bottle of wine, looked up as the young man spoke.

"I beg your pardon, Mr. Audley," he said, "but if you want to see your uncle, you'll lose your time by going to the Court just now. Sir Michael and my lady and Miss Alicia have all gone to the races up at Chorley, and they won't be back till nigh upon eight o'clock most likely. They must pass by here to go home."

Under these circumstances of course it was no use going to the Court, so the two young men strolled through the village and looked at the old church, and then went and reconnoitred the streams in which they were to fish the next day, and by such means beguiled the time till after seven o'clock. At about a quarter past that hour they returned to the inn, and seating themselves in the open window, lit their cigars and looked out at the peaceful prospect.

We hear every day of murders committed in
the country. Brutal and treacherous murders;
slow, protracted agonies from poisons administered
by some kindred hand; sudden and violent
deaths by cruel blows, inflicted with a stake cut
from some spreading oak, whose very shadow
promised—peace. In the county of which I write,
I have been shown a meadow in which, on a quiet
summer Sunday evening, a young farmer murdered the girl who had loved and trusted him;
and yet even now, with the stain of that foul
deed upon it, the aspect of the spot is—peace.
No crime has ever been committed in the worst
rookeries about Seven Dials that has not been also
done in the face of that sweet rustic calm which
still, in spite of all, we look on with a tender, half-
mournful yearning, and associate with—peace.

It was dusk when gigs and chaises, dogcarts
and clumsy farmers' phaetons, began to rattle
through the village street, and under the windows
of the Sun Inn; deeper dusk still when an open
carriage and four drew suddenly up beneath the
rocking sign-post.

It was Sir Michael Audley's barouche which came to so sudden a stop before the little inn. The harness of one of the leaders had become out of order, and the foremost postilion dismounted to set it right.

"Why, it's my uncle!" cried Robert Audley, as the carriage stopped. "I'll run down and speak to him."

George lit another cigar, and, sheltered by the window curtains, looked out at the little party. Alicia sat with her back to the horses, and he could perceive, even in the dusk, that she was a handsome brunette; but Lady Audley was seated on the side of the carriage furthest from the inn, and he could see nothing of the fair-haired paragon of whom he had heard so much.

"Why, Robert," exclaimed Sir Michael, as his nephew emerged from the inn, "this is a surprise!"

"I have not come to intrude upon you at the Court, my dear uncle," said the young man, as the baronet shook him by the hand in his own hearty fashion. "Essex is my native county, you

know, and about this time of year I generally
have a touch of home sickness; so George and I
have come down to the inn for two or three days'
fishing."

"George—George who?"

"George Talboys."

"What, has he come?" cried Alicia. "I'm so
glad; for I'm dying to see this handsome young
widower."

"Are you, Alicia?" said her cousin. "Then,
egad, I'll run and fetch him, and introduce you
to him at once."

Now, so complete was the dominion which
Lady Audley had, in her own childish, unthinking
way, obtained over her devoted husband, that
it was very rarely that the baronet's eyes were
long removed from his wife's pretty face. When
Robert, therefore, was about to re-enter the inn,
it needed but the faintest elevation of Lucy's
eyebrows, with a charming expression of weariness and terror, to make her husband aware that
she did not want to be bored by an introduction
to Mr. George Talboys.

"Never mind to-night, Bob," he said. "My wife is a little tired after our long day's pleasure. Bring your friend to dinner to-morrow, and then he and Alicia can make each other's acquaintance. Come round and speak to Lady Audley, and then we'll drive home."

My lady was so terribly fatigued that she could only smile sweetly, and hold out a tiny gloved hand to her nephew by marriage.

"You will come and dine with us to-morrow, and bring your interesting friend?" she said, in a low and tired voice. She had been the chief attraction of the race-course, and was wearied out by the exertion of fascinating half the county.

"It's a wonder she didn't treat you to her never-ending laugh," whispered Alicia, as she leant over the carriage door to bid Robert good night; "but I dare say she reserves that for your delectation to-morrow. "I suppose *you* are fascinated as well as everybody else?" added the young lady rather snappishly.

"She is a lovely creature, certainly," murmured Robert, with placid admiration.

"Oh, of course! Now, she is the first woman of whom I ever heard you say a civil word, Robert Audley. I'm sorry to find you can only admire wax dolls."

Poor Alicia had had many skirmishes with her cousin upon that peculiar temperament of his, which, while it enabled him to go through life with perfect content and tacit enjoyment, entirely precluded his feeling one spark of enthusiasm upon any subject whatever.

"As to his ever falling in love," thought the young lady sometimes, "the idea is too preposterous. If all the divinities upon earth were ranged before him, waiting for his sultanship to throw the handkerchief, he would only lift his eyebrows to the middle of his forehead, and tell them to scramble for it."

But, for once in his life, Robert was almost enthusiastic.

"She's the prettiest little creature you ever saw in your life, George," he cried, when the carriage had driven off and he returned to his friend. "Such blue eyes, such ringlets, such a ravishing

smile, such a fairy-like bonnet—all of a tremble
with heartsease and dewy spangles, shining out of
a cloud of gauze. George Talboys, I feel like the
hero of a French novel; I am falling in love with
my aunt."

The widower only sighed and puffed his cigar
fiercely out of the open window. Perhaps he was
thinking of that far-away time—little better than
five years ago, in fact; but such an age gone by
to him—when he first met the woman for whom
he had worn crape round his hat three days
before. They returned, all those old unforgotten
feelings; they came back, with the scene of their
birthplace. Again he lounged with his brother
officers upon the shabby pier at the shabby watering-place, listening to a dreary band with a cornet
that was a note and a half flat. Again he heard
the old operatic airs, and again *she* came tripping
towards him leaning on her old father's arm, and
pretending (with such a charming, delicious, serio-
comic pretence) to be listening to the music, and
quite unaware of the admiration of half a dozen
open-mouthed cavalry officers. Again the old

fancy came back that she was something too beautiful for earth, or earthly uses, and that to approach her was to walk in a higher atmosphere and to breathe a purer air. And since this she had been his wife, and the mother of his child. She lay in the little churchyard at Ventnor, and only a year ago he had given the order for her tombstone. A few slow, silent tears dropped upon his waistcoat as he thought of these things in the quiet and darkening room.

Lady Audley was so exhausted when she reached home, that she excused herself from the dinner-table, and retired at once to her dressing-room, attended by her maid, Phœbe Marks.

She was a little capricious in her conduct to this maid ; sometimes very confidential, sometimes rather reserved ; but she was a liberal mistress, and the girl had every reason to be satisfied with her situation.

This evening, in spite of her fatigue, she was in extremely high spirits, and gave an animated account of the races, and the company present at them.

"I am tired to death, though, Phœbe," she said by and by. "I'm afraid I must look a perfect fright, after a day in the hot sun."

There were lighted candles on each side of the glass before which Lady Audley was standing unfastening her dress. She looked full at her maid as she spoke, her blue eyes clear and bright, and the rosy, childish lips puckered into an arch smile.

"You are a little pale, my lady," answered the girl, "but you look as pretty as ever."

"That's right, Phœbe," she said, flinging herself into a chair and throwing back her curls at the maid, who stood, brush in hand, ready to arrange the luxuriant hair for the night. "Do you know, Phœbe, I have heard some people say you and I are alike?"

"I have heard them say so too, my lady," said the girl quietly, "but they must be very stupid to say it, for your ladyship is a beauty, and I'm a poor plain creature."

"Not at all, Phœbe," said the little lady superbly; "you *are* like me, and your features are very nice; it is only colour that you want. My

I 2

hair is pale yellow shot with gold, and yours is drab; my eyebrows and eyelashes are dark brown, and yours are almost—I scarcely like to say it, but they're almost white, my dear Phœbe; your complexion is sallow, and mine is pink and rosy. Why, with a bottle of hair dye, such as we see advertised in the papers, and a pot of rouge, you'd be as good-looking as I any day, Phœbe."

She prattled on in this way for a long time, talking of a hundred frivolous subjects, and ridiculing the people she had met at the races for her maid's amusement. Her step-daughter came into the dressing-room to bid her good night, and found the maid and mistress laughing aloud over one of the day's adventures. Alicia, who was never familiar with her servants, withdrew in disgust at my lady's frivolity.

"Go on brushing my hair, Phœbe," Lady Audley said, every time the girl was about to complete her task; "I quite enjoy a chat with you."

At last, just as she had dismissed her maid, she suddenly called her back. "Phœbe Marks," she said, "I want you to do me a favour."

"Yes, my lady."

"I want you to go to London by the first train to-morrow morning to execute a little commission for me. You may take a day's holiday afterwards, as I know you have friends in town, and I shall give you a five-pound note if you do what I want, and keep your own counsel about it."

"Yes, my lady."

"See that that door is securely shut, and come and sit on this stool at my feet."

The girl obeyed. Lady Audley smoothed her maid's neutral-tinted hair with her plump, white, and bejewelled hand as she reflected for a few moments.

"And now listen, Phœbe. What I want you to do is very simple."

It was so simple that it was told in five minutes, and then Lady Audley retired into her bed-room, and curled herself up cosily under the eider-down quilt. She was a chilly little creature, and loved to bury herself in soft wrappings of satin and fur.

"Kiss me, Phœbe," she said, as the girl

arranged the curtains. "I hear Sir Michael's
step in the anteroom; "you will meet him as you
go out, and you may as well tell him that you are
going up by the first train to-morrow morning to
get my dress from Madame Frederick for the
dinner at Morton Abbey."

It was late the next morning when Lady Audley
went down to breakfast—past ten o'clock. While
she was sipping her coffee a servant brought her
a sealed packet, and a book for her to sign.

"A telegraphic message!" she cried; for the
convenient word telegram had not yet been
invented. "What can be the matter?"

She looked up at her husband with wide-open,
terrified eyes, and seemed half afraid to break the
seal. The envelope was addressed to Miss Lucy
Graham, at Mr. Dawson's, and had been sent on
from the village.

"Read it, my darling," he said, "and do not
be alarmed; it may be nothing of any importance."

It came from a Mrs. Vincent, the schoolmistress
to whom she had referred on entering Mr. Daw-

son's family. The lady was dangerously ill, and implored her old pupil to go and see her.

"Poor soul! she always meant to leave me her money," said Lucy, with a mournful smile. "She has never heard of the change in my fortunes. Dear Sir Michael, I must go to her."

"To be sure you must, dearest. If she was kind to my poor girl in her adversity, she has a claim upon her prosperity that shall never be forgotten. Put on your bonnet, Lucy; we shall be in time to catch the express."

"You will go with me?"

"Of course, my darling. Do you suppose I would let you go alone?"

"I was sure you would go with me," she said thoughtfully.

"Does your friend send any address?"

"No; but she always lived at Crescent Villa, West Brompton; and no doubt she lives there still."

There was only time for Lady Audley to hurry on her bonnet and shawl before she heard the carriage drive round to the door, and Sir Michael calling to her at the foot of the staircase.

Her suite of rooms, as I have said, opened one out of another, and terminated in an octagon antechamber hung with oil paintings. Even in her haste she paused deliberately at the door of this room, double locked it, and dropped the key into her pocket. This door, once locked, cut off all access to my lady's apartments.

CHAPTER VIII.

BEFORE THE STORM.

So the dinner at Audley Court was postponed, and Miss Alicia had to wait still longer for an introduction to the handsome young widower, Mr. George Talboys.

I am afraid, if the real truth is to be told, there was, perhaps, something of affectation in the anxiety this young lady expressed to make George's acquaintance; but if poor Alicia for a moment calculated upon arousing any latent spark of jealousy lurking in her cousin's breast by this exhibition of interest, she was not so well acquainted with Robert Audley's disposition as she might have been. Indolent, handsome, and indifferent, the young barrister took life as altogether too absurd a mistake for any one event in its foolish course to be for a moment considered seriously by a sensible man.

His pretty, gipsy-faced cousin might have been over head and ears in love with him, and she might have told him so, in some charming, roundabout, womanly fashion, a hundred times in a day for all the three hundred and sixty-five days in the year; but unless she had waited for some privileged 29th of February, and walked straight up to him, saying, "Robert, please will you marry me?" I very much doubt if he would ever have discovered the state of her feelings.

Again, had he been in love with her himself, I fancy that the tender passion would, with him, have been so vague and feeble a sentiment that he might have gone down to his grave with a dim sense of some uneasy sensation which might be love or indigestion, and with, beyond this, no knowledge whatever of his state.

So it was not the least use, my poor Alicia, to ride about the lanes round Audley during those three days which the two young men spent in Essex; it was wasted trouble to wear that pretty cavalier hat and plume, and to be always, by the most singular of chances, meeting Robert and his friend. The black curls (nothing like Lady Audley's feathery ringlets, but heavy clustering locks, that clung about your slender brown throat), the red and pouting lips, the nose inclined to be *retroussé;* the dark complexion, with its bright crimson flush, always ready to glance up like a signal light in a dusky sky, when you came suddenly upon your apathetic cousin—all this coquettish, *espiègle,* brunette beauty was thrown away upon the dull eyes of Robert Audley, and you might as well have taken your rest in the cool drawing-room at the Court, instead of working your pretty mare to death under the hot September sun.

Now fishing, except to the devoted disciple of Izaac Walton, is not the most lively of occupations; therefore it is scarcely, perhaps, to be wondered that on the day after Lady Audley's departure, the two young men (one of whom was disabled, by that heart wound which he bore so quietly, from really taking pleasure in anything, and the other of whom looked upon almost all pleasure as a negative kind of trouble) began to grow weary of the shade of the willows overhanging the winding streams about Audley.

"Fig-tree Court is not gay in the long vacation," said Robert reflectively: "but I think, upon the whole, it's better than this; at any rate it's near a tobacconist's," he added, puffing resignedly at an execrable cigar procured from the landlord of the Sun Inn.

George Talboys, who had only consented to the Essex expedition in passive submission to his friend, was by no means inclined to object to their immediate return to London. "I shall be glad to get back, Bob," he said, "for I want to take a run down to Southampton; I haven't seen the little one for upwards of a month."

He always spoke of his son as "the little one;" always spoke of him mournfully rather than hopefully. It seemed as if he could take no comfort from the thought of his boy. He accounted for this by saying that he had a fancy that the child would never learn to love him; and worse even than this fancy, a dim presentiment that he would not live to see his little Georgey reach manhood.

"I'm not a romantic man, Bob," he would say sometimes, "and I never read a line of poetry in my life that was any more to me than so many words and so much jingle; but a feeling has come over me since my wife's death, that I am like a man standing upon a long low shore, with hideous cliffs frowning down upon him from behind, and the rising tide crawling slowly but surely about his feet. It seems to grow nearer and nearer every day, that black, pitiless tide; not rushing upon me with a great noise and a mighty impetus, but crawling, creeping, stealing, gliding towards me, ready to close in above my head when I am least prepared for the end."

Robert Audley stared at his friend in silent amazement; and, after a pause of profound deliberation, said solemnly, "George Talboys, I could understand this if you had been eating heavy suppers. Cold pork, now, especially if underdone, might produce this sort of thing. You want change of air, dear boy; you want the refreshing breezes of Fig-tree Court, and the soothing atmosphere of Fleet Street. Or, stay," he added suddenly; "I have it! You've been smoking our friend the landlord's cigars; that accounts for everything."

They met Alicia Audley on her mare about half an hour after they had come to the determination of leaving Essex early the next morning. The young lady was very much surprised and dis-appointed at hearing her cousin's determination, and for that very reason pretended to take the matter with supreme indifference.

"You are very soon tired of Audley, Robert," she said carelessly; "but of course you have no friends here, except your relations at the Court; while in London, no doubt, you have the most delightful society, and——"

"I get good tobacco," murmured Robert, inter-rupting his cousin. "Audley is the dearest old place, but when a man has to smoke dried cab-bage leaves, you know, Alicia——"

"Then you really are going to-morrow morn-ing?"

"Positively—by the express that leaves at 10·50."

"Then Lady Audley will lose an introduction to Mr. Talboys, and Mr. Talboys will lose the chance of seeing the prettiest woman in Essex."

"Really——" stammered George.

"The prettiest woman in Essex would have a poor chance of getting much admiration out of my friend, George Talboys," said Robert. "His heart is at Southampton, where he has a curly-headed little urchin, about as high as his knee, who calls him 'the big gentleman,' and asks him for sugar-plums."

"I am going to write to my step-mother by to-night's post," said Alicia. "She asked me particularly, in her letter, how long you were going to stop, and whether there was any chance of her being back in time to receive you."

Miss Audley took a letter from the pocket of her riding-jacket as she spoke—a pretty, fairy-like note, written on shining paper of a peculiar creamy hue.

"She says in her postscript, 'Be sure you answer my question about Mr. Audley and his friend, you volatile, forgetful Alicia!'"

" What a pretty hand she writes ! " said Robert, as his cousin folded the note.

"Yes, it is pretty, is it not ? Look at it, Robert."

She put the letter into his hand, and he contemplated it lazily for a few minutes, while Alicia patted the graceful neck of her chestnut mare, which was anxious to be off once more.

" Presently, Atalanta, presently. Give me back my note, Bob."

" It is the prettiest, most coquettish little hand I ever saw. Do you know, Alicia, I never believed in those fellows who ask you for thirteen postage stamps, and offer to tell you what you have never been able to find out yourself; but upon my word I think that if I had never seen your aunt, I should know what she was like by this slip of paper. Yes, here it all is—the feathery, gold-shot, flaxen curls, the pencilled eyebrows, the tiny straight nose, the winning childish smile, all to be guessed in these few graceful up-strokes and down-strokes. George, look here ! "

But absent-minded and gloomy George Talboys

had strolled away along the margin of a ditch, and· stood striking the bulrushes with his cane, half-a-dozen paces away from Robert and Alicia.

"Never mind," said the young lady impatiently; for she by no means relished this long disquisition upon my lady's little note. " Give me the letter, and let me go; it's past eight, and I must answer it by to-night's post. Come, Atalanta! Good-by, Robert—good-by, Mr. Talboys. A pleasant journey to town."

The chestnut mare cantered briskly through the lane, and Miss Audley was out of sight before those two big bright tears that stood in her eyes for one moment, before her pride sent them back again, rose from her angry heart.

"To have only one cousin in the world," she cried passionately, "my nearest relation after papa, and for him to care about as much for me as he would for a dog !"

By the merest of accidents, however, Robert and his friend did not go by the 10·50 express on the following morning, for the young barrister awoke with such a splitting headache, that he asked George to send him a cup of the strongest green tea that had ever been made at the Sun, and to be furthermore so good as to defer their journey until the next day. Of course George assented, and Robert Audley spent the forenoon lying in a darkened room, with a five-days'-old Chelmsford paper to entertain himself withal.

"It's nothing but the cigars, George," he said repeatedly. "Get me out of the place without my seeing the landlord; for if that man and I meet there will be bloodshed."

Fortunately for the peace of Audley, it happened to be market-day at Chelmsford; and the worthy landlord had ridden off in his chaise-cart to purchase supplies for his house—amongst other things, perhaps, a fresh stock of those very cigars which had been so fatal in their effect upon Robert.

The young men spent a dull, dawdling, stupid, unprofitable day; and towards dusk Mr. Audley proposed that they should stroll down to the Court, and ask Alicia to take them over the house.

"It will kill a couple of hours you know,

George; and it seems a great pity to drag you away from Audley without having shown you the old place, which I give you my honour is very well worth seeing."

The sun was low in the skies as they took a short cut through the meadows, and crossed a stile into the avenue leading to the archway— a lurid, heavy-looking, ominous sun-set, and a deathly stillness in the air, which frightened the birds that had a mind to sing, and left the field open to a few captious frogs croaking in the ditches. Still as the atmosphere was, the leaves rustled with that sinister, shivering motion which proceeds from no outer cause, but is rather an instinctive shudder of the frail branches, prescient of a coming storm. That stupid clock, which knew no middle course, and always skipped from one hour to the other, pointed to seven as the young men passed under the archway; but, for all that, it was nearer eight.

They found Alicia in the lime-walk, wandering listlessly up and down under the black shadow of the trees, from which every now

K 2

and then a withered leaf flapped slowly to the ground.

Strange to say, George Talboys, who very seldom observed anything, took particular notice of this place.

"It ought to be an avenue in a churchyard," he said. "How peacefully the dead might sleep under this sombre shade! I wish the churchyard at Ventnor was like this."

They walked on to the ruined well; and Alicia told them some old legend connected with the spot—some gloomy story, such as those always attached to an old house, as if the past were one dark page of sorrow and crime.

"We want to see the house before it is dark, Alicia," said Robert.

"Then we must be quick," she answered. "Come."

She led the way through an open French window, modernised a few years before, into the library, and thence to the hall.

In the hall they passed my lady's pale-faced

maid, who looked furtively under her white eye-lashes at the two young men.

They were going up-stairs, when Alicia turned and spoke to the girl.

"After we have been in the drawing-room I should like to show these gentlemen Lady Audley's rooms. Are they in good order, Phœbe?"

"Yes, Miss; but the door of the ante-room is locked, and I fancy that my lady has taken the key to London."

"Taken the key! Impossible!" cried Alicia.

"Indeed, Miss, I think she has. I cannot find it, and it always used to be in the door."

"I declare," said Alicia impatiently, "that it is not at all unlike my lady to have taken this silly freak into her head. I dare say she was afraid we should go into her rooms, and pry about amongst her pretty dresses, and meddle with her jewellery. It is very provoking, for the best pictures in the house are in that ante-chamber. There is her own portrait, too, unfinished, but wonderfully like.

"Her portrait!" exclaimed Robert Audley. "I would give anything to see it, for I have only an imperfect notion of her face. Is there no other way of getting into the room, Alicia?"

"Another way?"

"Yes; is there any door, leading through some of the other rooms, by which we can contrive to get into hers?"

His cousin shook her head, and conducted them into a corridor where there were some family portraits. She showed them a tapestried chamber, the large figures upon the faded canvas looking threatening in the dusky light.

"That fellow with the battle-axe looks as if he wanted to split George's head open," said Mr. Audley, pointing to a fierce warrior whose uplifted arm appeared above George Talboys' dark hair.

"Come out of this room, Alicia. I believe it's damp, or else haunted. Indeed I believe all ghosts to be the result of damp. You sleep in a damp bed—you awake suddenly in the dead of the night with a cold shiver, and see an old lady in the court costume of George the First's time, sitting at the foot of the bed. The old lady is indigestion, and the cold shiver is a damp sheet."

There were lighted candles in the drawing-room. No new-fangled lamps had ever made their appearance at Audley Court. Sir Michael's rooms were lighted by honest, thick, yellow-looking wax candles, in massive silver candlesticks, and in sconces against the walls.

There was very little to see in the drawing-room; and George Talboys soon grew tired of staring at the handsome modern furniture, and at a few pictures by some of the Academicians.

" Isn't there a secret passage, or an old oak chest, or something of that kind, somewhere about the place, Alicia?" asked Robert.

"To be sure !" cried Miss Audley; with a vehemence that startled her cousin; "of course. Why didn't I think of it before? How stupid of me, to be sure !"

" Why stupid ?"

" Because, if you don't mind crawling upon your hands and knees, you can see my lady's apartments, for that very passage communicates with her dressing-room. She doesn't know of it herself, I believe. How astonished she'd be if some black-visored burglar, with a dark lantern, were to rise through the floor some night as she sat before her looking-glass, having her hair dressed for a party!"

"Shall we try the secret passage, George?" asked Mr. Audley.

"Yes, if you wish it."

Alicia led them into the room which had once been her nursery. It was now disused, except on very rare occasions when the house was full of company.

Robert Audley lifted a corner of the carpet, according to his cousin's directions, and disclosed a rudely-cut trap-door in the oak flooring.

"Now listen to me," said Alicia. "You must let yourself down by your hands into the passage, which is about four feet high; stoop your head, and walk straight along it till you come to a sharp turn which will take you to the left, and at the extreme end of it you will find a short ladder below a trap-door like this, which you will have to unbolt; that door opens into the flooring of my lady's dressing-room, which is only covered with a square Persian carpet that you can easily manage to raise. You understand me?"

"Perfectly."

"Then take the light; Mr. Talboys will follow you. I give you twenty minutes for your inspection of the paintings—that is about a minute apiece—and at the end of that time I shall expect to see you return."

Robert obeyed her implicitly, and George, submissively following his friend, found himself, in five minutes, standing amidst the elegant disorder of Lady Audley's dressing-room.

She had left the house in a hurry on her unlooked-for journey to London, and the whole of her glittering toilette apparatus lay about on the marble dressing-table. The atmosphere of the room was almost oppressive from the rich odours of perfumes in bottles whose gold stoppers had not been replaced. A bunch of hothouse flowers was withering upon a tiny writing-table. Two or

three handsome dresses lay in a heap upon the
ground, and the open doors of a wardrobe revealed the treasures within. Jewellery, ivory-
backed hair-brushes, and exquisite china were
scattered here and there about the apartment.
George Talboys saw his bearded face and tall
gaunt figure reflected in the cheval-glass, and
wondered to see how out of place he seemed
among all these womanly luxuries.

They went from the dressing-room to the
boudoir, and through the boudoir into the ante-
chamber, in which there were, as Alicia had said,
about twenty valuable paintings besides my lady's
portrait.

My lady's portrait stood on an easel covered
with a green baize in the centre of the octagonal
chamber. It had been a fancy of the artist to
paint her standing in this very room, and to make
his background a faithful reproduction of the
pictured walls. I am afraid the young man
belonged to the pre-Raphaelite brotherhood, for
he had spent a most unconscionable time upon
the accessories of this picture—upon my lady's

crispy ringlets and the heavy folds of her crimson velvet dress.

The two young men looked at the paintings on the walls first, leaving this unfinished portrait for a *bonne bouche.*

By this time it was dark, the one candle carried by Robert only making one bright nucleus of light as he moved about holding it before the pictures one by one. The broad bare window looked out upon the pale sky, tinged with the last cold flicker of the dead twilight. The ivy rustled against the glass with the same ominous shiver as that which agitated every leaf in the garden, prophetic of the storm that was to come.

"There are our friend's eternal white horses," said Robert, stopping before a Wouvermans. "Nicholas Poussin—Salvator—ha—hum! Now for the portrait!"

He paused with his hand on the baize, and solemnly addressed his friend.

"George Talboys," he said, "we have between us only one wax candle, a very inadequate light

with which to look at a painting. Let me, therefore, request that you will suffer us to look at it
one at a time: if there is one thing more disagreeable than another, it is to have a person
dodging behind your back and peering over your
shoulder, when you're trying to see what a
picture's made of."

George fell back immediately. He took no
more interest in my lady's picture than in all the
other weariness of this troublesome world. He
fell back, and leaning his forehead against the
window-panes, looked out at the night.

When he turned round he saw that Robert had
arranged the easel very conveniently, and that he
had seated himself on a chair before it for the
purpose of contemplating the painting at his
leisure.

He rose as George turned round.

"Now, then, for your turn, Talboys," he said.
"It's an extraordinary picture."

He took George's place at the window, and
George seated himself in the chair before the easel.

Yes; the painter must have been a pre-

Raphaelite. No one but a pre-Raphaelite would have painted, hair by hair, those feathery masses of ringlets with every glimmer of gold, and every shadow of pale brown. No one but a pre-Raphaelite would have so exaggerated every attribute of that delicate face as to give a lurid lightness to the blonde complexion, and a strange, sinister light to the deep blue eyes. No one but a pre-Raphaelite could have given to that pretty pouting mouth the hard and almost wicked look it had in the portrait.

It was so like and yet so unlike; it was as if you had burned strange-coloured fires before my lady's face, and by their influence brought out new lines and new expressions never seen in it before. The perfection of feature, the brilliancy of colouring, were there; but I suppose the painter had copied quaint mediæval monstrosities until his brain had grown bewildered, for my lady, in his portrait of her, had something of the aspect of a beautiful fiend.

Her crimson dress, exaggerated like all the rest in this strange picture, hung about her in folds

that looked like flames, her fair head peeping out
of the lurid mass of colour, as if out of a raging
furnace.   Indeed, the crimson dress, the sunshine
on the face, the red gold gleaming in the yellow
hair, the ripe scarlet of the pouting lips, the
glowing colours of each accessory of the
minutely-painted background, all combined to
render the first effect of the painting by no
means an agreeable one.

But strange as the picture was, it could not
have made any great impression on George
Talboys, for he sat before it for about a quarter
of an hour without uttering a word—only staring
blankly at the painted canvas, with the candle-
stick grasped in his strong right hand, and his
left arm hanging loosely by his side.   He sat so
long in this attitude, that Robert turned round at
last.

"Why, George, I thought you had gone to
sleep!"

"I had almost."

"You've caught a cold from standing in that
damp tapestried room.   Mark my words, George

Talboys, you've caught a cold; you're as hoarse
as a raven. But come along."

Robert Audley took the candle from his friend's
hand, and crept back through the secret passage,
followed by George, very quiet, but scarcely more
quiet than usual.

They found Alicia in the nursery waiting for
them.

"Well?" she said interrogatively.

"We managed it capitally. But I don't like
the portrait; there's something odd about it."

"There is," said Alicia; "I've a strange fancy
on that point. I think that sometimes a painter
is in a manner inspired, and is able to see,
through the normal expression of the face,
another expression that is equally a part of it,
though not to be perceived by common eyes.
We have never seen my lady look as she does
in that picture; but I think that she *could*
look so."

"Alicia," said Robert Audley imploringly,
"don't be German!"

"But, Robert——"

"Don't be German, Alicia, if you love me.
The picture is—the picture; and my lady is—
my lady. That's my way of taking things, and
I'm not metaphysical; don't unsettle me."

He repeated this several times with an air of
terror perfectly sincere; and then, having
borrowed an umbrella in case of being over-
taken by the coming storm, left the Court,
leading passive George Talboys away with him.
The one hand of the stupid old clock had
skipped to nine by the time they reached the
archway; but before they could pass under
its shadow they had to step aside to allow
a carriage to dash by them. It was a fly from
the village, but Lady Audley's fair face peeped
out at the window. Dark as it was, she could
see the two figures of the young men black
against the dusk.

"Who is that?" she asked, putting out her
head. "Is it the gardener?"

"No, my dear aunt," said Robert, laughing;
"it is your most dutiful nephew."

He and George stopped by the archway while

the fly drew up at the door, and the surprised
servants came out to welcome their master and
mistress.

"I think the storm will hold off to-night,"
said the baronet, looking up at the sky; "but
we shall certainly have it to-morrow."

CHAPTER IX.

AFTER THE STORM.

Sir Michael was mistaken in his prophecy
upon the weather. The storm did not hold off
until next day, but burst with terrible fury over
the village of Audley about half an hour before
midnight.

Robert Audley took the thunder and lightning with the same composure with which he
accepted all the other ills of life. He lay on a
sofa in the sitting-room, ostensibly reading the
five-days'-old Chelmsford paper, and regaling
himself occasionally with a few sips from a large
tumbler of cold punch. But the storm had quite
a different effect upon George Talboys. His
friend was startled when he looked at the young
man's white face as he sat opposite the open
window listening to the thunder, and staring at

the black sky, rent every now and then by forked
streaks of steel-blue lightning.

"George," said Robert, after watching him
for some time, "are you frightened at the
lightning?"

"No," he answered curtly.

"But, my dear fellow, some of the most cour-
ageous men have been frightened at it. It is
scarcely to be called a fear; it is constitutional.
I am sure you are frightened at it."

"No, I am not."

"But, George, if you could see yourself, white
and haggard, with your great hollow eyes staring
out at the sky as if they were fixed upon a ghost.
I tell you I know that you are frightened."

"And I tell you that I am not."

"George Talboys, you are not only afraid of
the lightning, but you are savage with yourself
for being afraid, and with me for telling you of
your fear."

"Robert Audley, if you say another word to
me I shall knock you down;" having said which,
Mr. Talboys strode out of the room, banging the

door after him with a violence that shook the house. Those inky clouds which had shut in the sultry earth as if with a roof of hot iron, poured out their blackness in a sudden deluge as George left the room; but if the young man was afraid of the lightning, he certainly was not afraid of the rain; for he walked straight down stairs to the inn door, and went out into the wet high road. He walked up and down, up and down, in the soaking shower for about twenty minutes, and then, re-entering the inn, strode up to his bed-room.

Robert Audley met him on the landing, with his hair beaten about his white face, and his garments dripping wet.

"Are you going to bed, George?"

"Yes."

"But you have no candle."

"I don't want one."

"But look at your clothes, man! Do you see the wet streaming down your coat-sleeves? What on earth made you go out upon such a night?"

"I am tired, and want to go to bed—don't bother me."

"You'll take some hot brandy-and-water, George?"

Robert Audley stood in his friend's way as he spoke, anxious to prevent his going to bed in the state he was in; but George pushed him fiercely aside, and striding past him, said, in the same hoarse voice Robert had noticed at the Court—

"Let me alone, Robert Audley, and keep clear of me if you can."

Robert followed George to his bed-room, but the young man banged the door in his face; so there was nothing for it but to leave Mr. Talboys to himself, to recover his temper as best he might.

"He was irritated at my noticing his terror at the lightning," thought Robert, as he calmly retired to rest, serenely indifferent to the thunder which seemed to shake him in his bed, and the lightning playing fitfully round the razors in his open dressing-case.

The storm rolled away from the quiet village of Audley, and when Robert awoke the next morning it was to see bright sunshine, and a peep of cloudless sky between the white curtains of his bed-room window.

It was one of those serene and lovely mornings that sometimes succeed a storm. The birds sung loud and cheerily, the yellow corn uplifted itself in the broad fields, and waved proudly after its sharp tussle with the storm, which had done its best to beat down the heavy ears with cruel wind and driving rain half the night through. The vine-leaves clustering round Robert's window fluttered with a joyous rustling, shaking the rain-drops in diamond showers from every spray and tendril.

Robert Audley found his friend waiting for him at the breakfast-table.

George was very pale, but perfectly tranquil — if anything, indeed, more cheerful than usual.

He shook Robert by the hand with something of that old hearty manner for which he had been

distinguished before the one affliction of his life
overtook and shipwrecked him.

"Forgive me, Bob," he said frankly, "for
my surly temper of last night.   You were quite
correct in your assertion; the thunder-storm
did upset me.   It always had the same effect
upon me in my youth."

"Poor old boy!   Shall we go up by the
express, or shall we stop here and dine with my
uncle to-night?" asked Robert.

"To tell the truth, Bob, I would rather do
neither.   It's a glorious morning.   Suppose we
stroll about all day, take another turn with
the rod and line, and go up to town by
the train that leaves here at 6.15 in the
evening?"

Robert Audley would have assented to a far
more disagreeable proposition than this, rather
than have taken the trouble to oppose his friend,
so the matter was immediately agreed upon;
and after they had finished their breakfast, and
ordered a four-o'clock dinner, George Talboys
took the fishing-rod across his broad shoulders,

and strode out of the house with his friend and companion.

But if the equable temperament of Mr. Robert Audley had been undisturbed by the crackling peals of thunder that shook the very foundations of the Sun Inn, it had not been so with the more delicate sensibilities of his uncle's young wife. Lady Audley confessed herself terribly frightened of the lightning. She had her bedstead wheeled into a corner of the room, and with the heavy curtains drawn tightly round her, she lay with her face buried in the pillows, shuddering convulsively at every sound of the tempest without. Sir Michael, whose stout heart had never known a fear, almost trembled for this fragile creature, whom it was his happy privilege to protect and defend. My lady would not consent to undress till nearly three o'clock in the morning, when the last lingering peal of thunder had died away amongst the distant hills. Until that hour she lay in the handsome silk dress in which she had travelled, huddled together, amongst the bed-clothes, only looking up now and then with a scared face to ask if the storm was over.

Towards four o'clock, her husband, who spent the night in watching by her bed-side, saw her drop off into a deep sleep, from which she did not awake for nearly five hours.

But she came into the breakfast-room, at half-past nine o'clock, singing a little Scotch melody, her cheeks tinged with as delicate a pink as the pale hue of her muslin morning dress. Like the birds and the flowers, she seemed to recover her beauty and joyousness in the morning sunshine. She tripped lightly out on to the lawn, gathering a last lingering rosebud here and there, and a sprig or two of geranium, and returning through the dewy grass, warbling long cadences for very happiness of heart, and looking as fresh and radiant as the flowers in her hands. The baronet caught her in his strong arms as she came in through the open window.

"My pretty one," he said, "my darling, what happiness to see you your own merry self again!

Do you know, Lucy, that once last night, when
you looked out through the dark green bed-
curtains, with your poor white face, and the
purple rims round your hollow eyes, I had
almost a difficulty to recognise my little wife
in that ghastly, terrified, agonised-looking creature, crying out about the storm. Thank God
for the morning sun, which has brought back
the rosy cheeks and the bright smile! I hope
to Heaven, Lucy, I shall never again see you
look as you did last night."

She stood on tiptoe to kiss him, and was
then only tall enough to reach his white beard.
She told him, laughing, that she had always been
a silly, frightened creature,—frightened of dogs,
frightened of cattle, frightened of a thunder-
storm, frightened of a rough sea. "Frightened
of everything and everybody, but my dear,
noble, handsome husband," she said.

She had found the carpet in her dressing-room
disarranged, and had inquired into the mystery
of the secret passage. She chid Miss Alicia
in a playful, laughing way, for her boldness

in introducing two great men into my lady's rooms.

"And they had the audacity to look at my picture, Alicia," she said, with mock indignation. "I found the baize thrown on the ground, and a great man's glove on the carpet. Look!"

She held up a thick driving-glove as she spoke. It was George's, which he had dropped while looking at the picture.

"I shall go up to the Sun, and ask those boys to dinner," Sir Michael said, as he left the Court upon his morning walk round his farm.

Lady Audley flitted from room to room in the bright September sunshine—now sitting down to the piano to trill out a ballad, or the first page of an Italian bravura, or running with rapid fingers through a brilliant waltz— now hovering about a stand of hothouse flowers, doing amateur gardening with a pair of fairy-like silver-mounted embroidery scissors—now strolling into her dressing-room to talk to Phœbe Marks, and have her curls re-arranged for the third or fourth time; for the ringlets were always getting into disorder, and gave no little trouble to Lady Audley's maid.

My lady seemed, on this particular September day, restless from very joyousness of spirit, and unable to stay long in one place, or occupy herself with one thing.

While Lady Audley amused herself in her own frivolous fashion, the two young men strolled slowly along the margin of a stream until they reached a shady corner where the water was deep and still, and the long branches of the willows trailed into the brook.

George Talboys took the fishing-rod, while Robert stretched himself at full length on a railway rug, and balancing his hat upon his nose as a screen from the sunshine, fell fast asleep.

Those were happy fish in the stream on the banks of which Mr. Talboys was seated. They might have amused themselves to their heart's content with timid nibbles at this gentleman's bait, without in any manner endangering their safety; for George only stared vacantly at the water, holding

his rod in a loose, listless hand, and with a
strange far-away look in his eyes. As the church
clock struck two he threw down his rod, and
striding away along the bank, left Robert Audley
to enjoy a nap, which, according to that gentleman's habits, was by no means unlikely to last
for two or three hours. About a quarter of a
mile further on George crossed a rustic bridge,
and struck into the meadows which led to Audley
Court.

The birds had sung so much all the morning
that they had, perhaps, by this time grown
tired; the lazy cattle were asleep in the meadows; Sir Michael was still away on his morning's ramble; Miss Alicia had scampered off an
hour before upon her chestnut mare; the servants
were all at dinner in the back part of the house;
and my lady had strolled, book in hand, into the
shadowy lime-walk; so the grey old building
had never worn a more peaceful aspect than on
that bright afternoon when George Talboys
walked across the lawn to ring a sonorous peal
at the sturdy, iron-bound oak door.

The servant who answered his summons told him that Sir Michael was out, and my lady walking in the lime-tree avenue.

He looked a little disappointed at this intelligence, and muttering something about wishing to see my lady, or going to look for my lady (the servant did not clearly distinguish his words), strode away from the door without leaving either card or message for the family.

It was full an hour and a half after this when Lady Audley returned to the house, not coming from the lime-walk, but from exactly the opposite direction, carrying her open book in her hand, and singing as she came. Alicia had just dismounted from her mare, and stood in the low-arched doorway, with her great Newfoundland dog by her side.

The dog, which had never liked my lady, showed his teeth with a suppressed growl.

"Send that horrid animal away, Alicia," Lady Audley said impatiently. "The brute knows that I am frightened of him, and takes advantage of my terror. And yet they call the creatures generous and noble-natured! Bah, Cæsar; I hate you, and you hate me; and if you met me in the dark in some narrow passage you would fly at my throat and strangle me, wouldn't you?"

My lady, safely sheltered behind her step-daughter, shook her yellow curls at the angry animal, and defied him maliciously.

"Do you know, Lady Audley, that Mr. Talboys, the young widower, has been here asking for Sir Michael and for you?"

Lucy Audley lifted her pencilled eyebrows. "I thought he was coming to dinner," she said. "Surely we shall have enough of him then."

She had a heap of wild autumn flowers in the skirt of her muslin dress. She had come through the fields at the back of the Court, gathering the hedge-row blossoms in her way. She ran lightly up the broad staircase to her own rooms. George's glove lay on her boudoir table. Lady Audley rang the bell violently, and it was answered by Phœbe Marks. "Take that litter away," she said sharply. The girl collected the glove and a few withered flowers and torn papers lying on the table into her apron.

"What have you been doing all this morning?" asked my lady. "Not wasting your time, I hope?"

"No, my lady, I have been altering the blue dress. It is rather dark on this side of the house, so I took it up to my own room, and worked at the window."

The girl was leaving the room as she spoke, but she turned round and looked at Lady Audley as if waiting for further orders.

Lucy looked up at the same moment, and the eyes of the two women met.

"Phœbe Marks," said my lady, throwing herself into an easy chair, and trifling with the wild flowers in her lap, "you are a good industrious girl, and while I live and am prosperous you shall never want a firm friend or a twenty-pound note."

CHAPTER X.

MISSING.

WHEN Robert Audley awoke he was surprised to see the fishing-rod lying on the bank, the line trailing idly in the water, and the float bobbing harmlessly up and down in the afternoon sunshine. The young barrister was a long time stretching his arms and legs in various directions to convince himself, by means of such exercise, that he still retained the proper use of those members; then, with a mighty effort, he contrived to rise from the grass, and having deliberately folded his railway rug into a convenient s ape for carrying over his shoulder, he strolled away to look for George Talboys.

Once or twice he gave a sleepy shout, scarcely loud enough to scare the birds in the branches above his head, or the trout in the stream at his feet; but receiving no answer, grew tired of the exertion, and dawdled on, yawning as he went, and still looking for George Talboys.

By-and-by he took out his watch, and was surprised to, find that it was a quarter past four.

" Why, the selfish beggar must have gone home to his dinner ! " he muttered reflectively ; " and yet that isn't much like him, for he seldom remembers even his meals unless I jog his memory."

Even a good appetite, and the knowledge that his dinner would very likely suffer by this delay, could not quicken Mr. Robert Audley's constitutional dawdle, and by the time he strolled in at the front door of the Sun the clocks were striking five. He so fully expected to find George Talboys waiting for him in the little sitting-room, that the absence of that gentleman seemed to give the apartment a dreary look, and Robert groaned aloud.

" This is lively ! " he said. " A cold dinner, and nobody to eat it with ! "

The landlord of the Sun came himself to apologise for his ruined dishes.

" As fine a pair of ducks, Mr. Audley, as ever you clapped eyes on, but burnt up to a cinder, along of being kep' hot."

" Never mind the ducks," Robert said, impatiently ; " where's Mr. Talboys ? "

" He ain't been in, sir, since you went out together this morning."

" What ! " cried Robert. " Why, in Heaven's name, what has the man done with himself ? "

He walked to the window and looked out upon the broad white high road. There was a waggon laden with trusses of hay crawling slowly past, the lazy horses and the lazy waggoner dropping their heads with a weary stoop under the afternoon sunshine. There was a flock of sheep straggling about the road, with a dog running himself into a fever in the endeavour to keep them decently together. There were some bricklayers just released from work—a tinker mending some kettles by the road-side ; there was a dogcart dashing down the road, carrying the master

of the Audley hounds to his seven o'clock dinner·
there were a dozen common village sights and
sounds that mixed themselves up into a cheerful
bustle and confusion; but there was no George
Talboys.

"Of all the extraordinary things that ever
happened to me in the whole course of my life,"
said Mr. Robert Audley, "this is the most
miraculous !"

The landlord, still in attendance, opened his
eyes as Robert made this remark. What could
there be so extraordinary in the simple fact of a
gentleman being late for his dinner?

"I shall go and look for him," said Robert,
snatching up his hat and walking straight out of
the house.

But the question was where to look for him.
He certainly was not by the trout stream, so it
was no good going back there in search of him.
Robert was standing before the inn, deliberating
on what was best to be done, when the landlord
came out after him.

"I forgot to tell you, Mr. Audley, as how your

uncle called here five minutes after you was
gone, and left a message asking of you and the
other gentleman to go down to dinner at the
Court."

"Then I shouldn't wonder," said Robert, "if
George Talboys has gone down to the Court to
call upon my uncle. It isn't like him, but it's
just possible that he has done it."

It was six o'clock when Robert knocked at the
door of his uncle's house. He did not ask to see
any of the family, but inquired at once for his
friend.

Yes, the servant told him; Mr. Talboys had
been there at two o'clock, or a little after.

"And not since?"

"No, not since."

Was the man sure that it was at two Mr.
Talboys called? Robert asked.

Yes, perfectly sure. He remembered the hour
because it was the servants' dinner hour, and he
had left the table to open the door to Mr.
Talboys.

"Why, what can have become of the man?"

thought Robert, as he turned his back upon the
Court. "From two till six—four good hours—
and no signs of him!"

If any one had ventured to tell Mr. Robert
Audley that he could possibly feel a strong attachment to any creature breathing, that cynical
gentleman would have elevated his eyebrows in
supreme contempt at the preposterous notion.
Yet here he was, flurried and anxious, bewildering
his brain by all manner of conjectures about his
missing friend, and, false to every attribute of his
nature, walking fast.

"I haven't walked fast since I was at Eton,"
he murmured, as he hurried across one of Sir
Michael's meadows in the direction of the village;
"and the worst of it is that I haven't the most
remote idea where I am going."

He crossed another meadow, and then seating himself upon a stile, rested his elbows upon
his knees, buried his face in his hands, and set
himself seriously to think the matter out.

"I have it!" he said, after a few minutes'
thought; "the railway station!"   He sprang

over the stile, and started off in the direction of the little red brick building.

There was no train expected for another half hour, and the clerk was taking his tea in an apartment on one side of the office, on the door of which was inscribed, in large white letters, "Private."

But Mr. Audley was too much occupied with the one idea of looking for his friend to pay any attention to this warning. He strode at once to the door, and rattling his cane against it, brought the clerk out of his sanctum in a perspiration from hot tea, and with his mouth full of bread and butter.

"Do you remember the gentleman that came down to Audley with me, Smithers?" asked Robert.

"Well, to tell you the real truth, Mr. Audley, I can't say I do. You came by the four o'clock, if you remember, and there's always a many by that train."

"You don't remember him, then?"

"Not to my knowledge, sir."

"That's provoking! I want to know, Smithers, whether he has taken a ticket for London since two o'clock to-day. He's a tall, broad-chested young fellow, with a big brown beard. You couldn't well mistake him."

"There was four or five gentlemen as took tickets for the 3·30 up," said the clerk rather vaguely, casting an anxious glance over his shoulder at his wife, who looked by no means pleased at this interruption to the harmony of the tea-table.

"Four or five gentlemen! But did either of them answer to the description of my friend?"

"Well, I think one of them had a beard, sir."

"A dark brown beard?"

"Well, I don't know but what it was brownish like."

"Was he dressed in grey?"

"I believe it was grey: a many gents wears grey. He asked for the ticket sharp and short like, and when he'd got it walked straight out on to the platform whistling."

"That's George!" said Robert. "Thank you, Smithers: I needn't trouble you any more. It's as clear as daylight," he muttered, as he left the station, "he's got one of his gloomy fits on him, and he's gone back to London without saying a word about it. I'll leave Audley myself to-morrow morning; and for to-night—why, I may as well go down to the Court, and make the acquaintance of my uncle's young wife. They don't dine till seven: if I get back across the fields I shall be in time. Bob—otherwise Robert Audley, this sort of thing will never do: you are falling over head and ears in love with your aunt."

CHAPTER XI.

THE MARK UPON MY LADY'S WRIST.

ROBERT found Sir Michael and Lady Audley in the drawing-room. My lady was sitting on a music-stool before the grand piano, turning over the leaves of some new music. She twirled round upon this revolving seat, making a rustling with her silk flounces, as Mr. Robert Audley's name was announced; then, leaving the piano, she made her nephew a pretty mock ceremonious curtsey. "Thank you so much for the sables," she said, holding out her little fingers, all glittering and twinkling with the diamonds she wore upon them; "thank you for those beautiful sables. How good it was of you to get them for me!"

Robert had almost forgotten the commission he had executed for Lady Audley during his Russian expedition. His mind was so full of George

Talboys that he only acknowledged my lady's gratitude by a bow.

"Would you believe it, Sir Michael?" he said. "That foolish chum of mine has gone back to London, leaving me in the lurch."

"Mr. George Talboys returned to town!" exclaimed my lady, lifting her eyebrows.

"What a dreadful catastrophe!" said Alicia maliciously, "since Pythias, in the person of Mr. Robert Audley, cannot exist for half an hour without Damon, commonly known as George Talboys."

"He's a very good fellow," Robert said stoutly; "and to tell the honest truth, I'm rather uneasy about him."

Uneasy about him! My lady was quite anxious to know why Robert was uneasy about his friend.

"I'll tell you why, Lady Audley," answered the young barrister. "George had a bitter blow a year ago in the death of his wife. He has never got over that trouble. He takes life pretty quietly —almost as quietly as I do—but he often talks very strangely, and I sometimes think that one day this grief will get the better of him, and he'll do something rash."

Mr. Robert Audley spoke vaguely; but all three of his listeners knew that the something rash to which he alluded was that one deed for which there is no repentance.

There was a brief pause, during which Lady Audley arranged her yellow ringlets by the aid of the glass over the console table opposite to her.

"Dear me!" she said, "this is very strange. I did not think men were capable of these deep and lasting affections. I thought that one pretty face was as good as another pretty face to them, and that when number one with blue eyes and fair hair died, they had only to look out for number two with black eyes and hair, by way of variety."

"George Talboys is not one of those men. I firmly believe that his wife's death broke his heart."

"How sad!" murmured Lady Audley. "It seems almost cruel of Mrs. Talboys to die, and grieve her poor husband so much."

"Alicia was right; she *is* childish," thought Robert, as he looked at his aunt's pretty face.

My lady was very charming at the dinner-table; she professed the most bewitching incapacity for carving the pheasant set before her, and called Robert to her assistance.

"I could carve a leg of mutton at Mr. Dawson's," she said, laughing; "but a leg of mutton is so easy; and then I used to stand up."

Sir Michael watched the impression my lady made upon his nephew with a proud delight in her beauty and fascination.

"I am so glad to see my poor little woman in her usual good spirits once more," he said. "She was very down-hearted yesterday at a disappointment she met with in London."

"A disappointment!"

"Yes, Mr. Audley, a very cruel one," answered my lady. "I received the other morning a telegraphic message from my dear old friend and schoolmistress, telling me that she was dying, and that if I wanted to see her again I must hasten to her immediately. The telegraphic despatch contained no address, and of course, from that very circumstance, I imagined that she must be living in the house in which I left her three years ago. Sir Michael and I hurried up to town immediately, and drove straight to the old address. The house was occupied by strange people, who could give me no tidings of my friend. It is in a retired place, where there are a very few tradespeople about. Sir Michael made inquiries at the few shops there are, but, after taking an immense deal of trouble, could discover nothing whatever likely to lead to the information we wanted. I have no friends in London, and had therefore no one to assist me except my dear, generous husband, who did all in his power, but in vain, to find my friend's new residence."

"It was very foolish not to send the address in the telegraphic message," said Robert.

"When people are dying it is not so easy to think of all these things," murmured my lady, looking reproachfully at Mr. Audley with her soft blue eyes.

In spite of Lady Audley's fascination, and in spite of Robert's very unqualified admiration of her, the barrister could not overcome a vague feeling of uneasiness on this quiet September evening.

As he sat in the deep embrasure of a mullioned window, talking to my lady, his mind wandered away to shady Fig-tree Court, and he thought of poor George Talboys smoking his solitary cigar in the room with the dogs and the canaries. " I wish I'd never felt any friendliness for the fellow," he thought. " I feel like a man who has an only son whose life has gone wrong with him. I wish to Heaven I could give him back his wife, and send him down to Ventnor to finish his days in peace."

Still my lady's pretty musical prattle ran on as merrily and continuously as the babble of some brook; and still Robert's thoughts wandered, in spite of himself, to George Talboys.

He thought of him hurrying down to Southampton by the mail train to see his boy. He thought of him as he had often seen him, spelling over the shipping advertisements in the *Times*, looking for a vessel to take him back to Australia. Once he thought of him with a shudder, lying cold and stiff at the bottom of some shallow stream, with his dead face turned towards the darkening sky.

Lady Audley noticed his abstraction, and asked him what he was thinking of.

"George Talboys," he answered abruptly.

She gave a little nervous shudder.

"Upon my word," she said, "you make me quite uncomfortable by the way in which you talk of Mr. Talboys. One would think that something extraordinary had happened to him."

"God forbid! But I cannot help feeling uneasy about him."

Later in the evening Sir Michael asked for some music, and my lady went to the piano. Robert Audley strolled after her to the instrument to turn over the leaves of her music; but she played from memory, and he was spared the trouble his gallantry would have imposed upon him.

He carried a pair of lighted candles to the
piano, and arranged them conveniently for the
pretty musician. She struck a few chords, and
then wandered into a pensive sonata of Beethoven's. It was one of the many paradoxes
in her character, that love of sombre and melancholy melodies, so opposite to her gay, frivolous
nature.

Robert Audley lingered by her side, and as he
had no occupation in turning over the leaves of
her music, he amused himself by watching her
jewelled white hands gliding softly over the keys,
with the lace sleeves dropping away from her
graceful arched wrists. He looked at her pretty
fingers one by one; this one glittering with a ruby
heart; that encoiled by an emerald serpent; and
about them all a starry glitter of diamonds.
From the fingers his eyes wandered to the rounded
wrists: the broad, flat, gold bracelet upon her
right wrist dropped over her hand, as she executed
a rapid passage. She stopped abruptly to re-
arrange it; but before she could do so, Robert
Audley noticed a bruise upon her delicate skin.

"You have hurt your arm, Lady Audley," he exclaimed.

She hastily replaced the bracelet.

"It is nothing," she said. "I am unfortunate in having a skin which the slightest touch bruises."

She went on playing, but Sir Michael came across the room to look into the matter of the bruise upon his wife's pretty wrist.

"What is it, Lucy?" he asked; "and how did it happen?"

"How foolish you all are to trouble yourselves about anything so absurd!" said Lady Audley, laughing. "I am rather absent in mind, and amused myself a few days ago by tying a piece of ribbon round my arm so tightly, that it left a bruise when I removed it."

"Hum!" thought Robert. "My lady tells little childish white lies; the bruise is of a more recent date than a few days ago; the skin has only just begun to change colour."

Sir Michael took the slender wrist in his strong hand.

" Hold the candles, Robert," he said, " and let us look at this poor little arm."

It was not one bruise, but four slender, purple marks, such as might have been made by the four fingers of a powerful hand that had grasped the delicate wrist a shade too roughly. A narrow ribbon, bound tightly, might have left some such marks, it is true, and my lady protested once more that, to the best of her recollection, that must have been how they were made.

Across one of the faint purple marks there was a darker tinge, as if a ring worn on one of these strong and cruel fingers had been ground into the tender flesh.

"I am sure my lady must tell white lies," thought Robert, "for I can't believe the story of the ribbon."

He wished his relations good night and good-by at about half-past ten o'clock; he said that he should run up to London by the first train to look for George, in Fig-tree Court.

" If I don't find him there, I shall go to South-ampton," he said; " and if I don't find him there——"

"What then?" asked my lady.

"I shall think that something strange has happened."

Robert Audley felt very low-spirited as he walked slowly home between the shadowy meadows; more low-spirited still when he re-entered the sitting-room at the Sun Inn, where he and George had lounged together, staring out of the window, and smoking their cigars.

"To think," he said, meditatively, "that it is possible to care so much for a fellow! But come what may, I'll go up to town after him the first thing to-morrow morning, and sooner than be balked in finding him, I'll go to the very end of the world."

With Mr. Robert Audley's lymphatic nature, determination was so much the exception, rather than the rule, that when he did for once in his life resolve upon any course of action, he had a certain dogged, iron-like obstinacy that pushed him on to the fulfilment of his purpose.

The lazy bent of his mind, which prevented him from thinking of half a dozen things at a time, and not thinking thoroughly of any one of them, as is the manner of your more energetic people, made him remarkably clear-sighted upon any point to which he ever gave his serious attention.

Indeed, after all, though solemn benchers laughed at him, and rising barristers shrugged their shoulders under rustling silk gowns when people spoke of Robert Audley, I doubt if, had he ever taken the trouble to get a brief, he might not have rather surprised the magnates who underrated his abilities.

CHAPTER XII.

STILL MISSING.

THE September sun-light sparkled upon the
fountain in the Temple Gardens, when Robert
Audley returned to Fig-tree Court early the following morning.

He found the canaries singing in the pretty
little room in which George had slept, but the
apartment was in the same prim order in which
the laundress had arranged it after the departure
of the two young men—not a chair displaced, or
so much as the lid of a cigar-box lifted, to bespeak
the presence of George Talboys. With a last
lingering hope he searched upon the mantel-pieces
and tables of his rooms, on the chance of finding
some letter left by George.

"He may have slept here last night, and
started for Southampton early this morning,

he thought. " Mrs. Maloney has been here very likely, to make everything tidy after him."

But as he sat looking lazily round the room, now and then whistling to his delighted canaries, a slip-shod foot upon the staircase without bespoke the advent of that very Mrs. Maloney who waited upon the two young men.

No, Mr. Talboys had not come home ; she had looked in as early as six o'clock that morning, and found the chambers empty.

Had anything happened to the poor dear gentleman ? she asked, seeing Robert Audley's pale face.

He turned round upon her quite savagely at this question.

Happened to him ! What should happen to him ? They had only parted at two o'clock the day before.

Mrs. Maloney would have related to him the history of a poor dear young engine-driver, who had once lodged with her, and who went out, after eating a hearty dinner, in the best of spirits, to meet with his death from the concussion of an express and a luggage train; but Robert put on his hat again, and walked straight out of the house, before the honest Irishwoman could begin her pitiful story.

It was growing dusk when he reached South-ampton. He knew his way to the poor little ter-race of houses, in a dull street leading down to the water, where George's father-in-law lived. Little Georgey was playing at the open parlour window as the young man walked down the street.

Perhaps it was this fact, and the dull and silent aspect of the house, which filled Robert Audley's mind with a vague conviction that the man he came to look for was not there. The old man himself opened the door, and the child peeped out of the parlour to look at the strange gentle-man.

He was a handsome boy, with his father's brown eyes and dark waving hair, and yet with some latent expression which was not his father's, and which pervaded his whole face, so that although each feature of the child resembled the same feature in George Talboys, the boy was not actually like him.

The old man was delighted to see Robert Audley; he remembered having had the pleasure of meeting him at Ventnor, on the melancholy occasion of —— He wiped his watery old eyes by way of conclusion to the sentence. Would Mr. Audley walk in? Robert strode into the little parlour. The furniture was shabby and dingy, and the place reeked with the smell of stale tobacco and brandy-and-water. The boy's broken playthings and the old man's broken clay pipes, and torn, brandy-and-water stained newspapers, were scattered upon the dirty carpet. Little Georgey crept towards the visitor, watching him furtively out of his big brown eyes. Robert took the boy on his knee, and gave him his watch-chain to play with while he talked to the old man.

"I need scarcely ask the question that I came to ask," he said. "I was in hopes I should have found your son-in-law here."

"What! you knew that he was coming to Southampton?"

"Knew that he was coming!" cried Robert, brightening up. "He *is* here, then?"

"No, he is not here now, but he has been here."

"When?"

"Late last night; he came by the mail."

"And left again immediately?"

"He stayed little better than an hour."

"Good heavens!" said Robert, "what useless anxiety that man has given me! What can be the meaning of all this?"

"You knew nothing of his intention, then?"

"Of what intention?"

"I mean of his determination to go to Australia."

"I knew that it was always in his mind more or less, but not more just now than usual."

"He sails to-night from Liverpool. He came here at one o'clock this morning to have a look at the boy, he said, before he left England, perhaps never to return. He told me he was sick of

the world, and that the rough life out there was
the only thing to suit him. He stayed an hour,
kissed the boy, without awaking him, and left
Southampton by the mail that starts at a quarter
past two."

"What can be the meaning of all this?" said
Robert. "What could be his motive for leaving
England in this manner, without a word to me,
his most intimate friend—without even a change
of clothes; for he has left everything at my
chambers? It is the most extraordinary pro-
ceeding!"

The old man looked very grave. "Do you
know, Mr. Audley," he said, tapping his forehead
significantly, "I sometimes fancy that Helen's
death had a strange effect upon poor George."

"Pshaw!" cried Robert contemptuously; "he
felt the blow most cruelly, but his brain was as
sound as yours or mine."

"Perhaps he will write to you from Liverpool,"
said George's father-in-law. He seemed anxious
to smooth over any indignation that Robert might
feel at his friend's conduct.

"He ought," said Robert gravely, "for we've been good friends from the days when we were together at Eton. It isn't kind of George Talboys to treat me like this."

But even at the moment that he uttered the reproach a strange thrill of remorse shot through his heart.

"It isn't like him," he said, "it isn't like George Talboys"

Little Georgey caught at the sound. "That's my name," he said, "and my papa's name—the big gentleman's name."

"Yes, little Georgey, and your papa came last night and kissed you in your sleep. Do you remember ?"

"No," said the boy, shaking his curly little head.

"You must have been very fast asleep, little Georgey, not to see poor papa."

The child did not answer, but presently, fixing his eyes upon Robert's face, he said abruptly,—

"Where's the pretty lady ? "

"What pretty lady ? "

"The pretty lady that used to come a long while
ago."

"He means his poor mamma," said the old
man.

"No," cried the boy resolutely, "not mamma.
Mamma was always crying. I didn't like mamma——"

"Hush, little Georgey!"

"But I didn't, and she didn't like me. She
was always crying. I mean the pretty lady; the
lady that was dressed so fine, and that gave me
my gold watch."

"He means the wife of my old captain—an
excellent creature, who took a great fancy to
Georgey, and gave him some handsome presents."

"Where's my gold watch? Let me show the
gentleman my gold watch," cried Georgey.

"It's gone to be cleaned, Georgey," answered
his grandfather.

"It's always going to be cleaned," said the
boy.

"The watch is perfectly safe, I assure you, Mr.
Audley," murmured the old man, apologetically;

and taking out a pawnbroker's duplicate, he handed it to Robert.

It was made out in the name of Captain Mortimer: "Watch, set with diamonds, £11."

"I'm often hard pressed for a few shillings, Mr. Audley," said the old man. "My son-in-law has been very liberal to me; but there are others, there are others, Mr. Audley—and—and—I've not been treated well." He wiped away some genuine tears as he said this in a pitiful, crying voice. "Come, Georgey, it's time the brave little man was in bed. Come along with grandpapa. Excuse me for a quarter of an hour, Mr. Audley."

The boy went very willingly. At the door of the room the old man looked back at his visitor, and said, in the same peevish voice, "This is a poor place for me to pass my declining years in, Mr. Audley. I've made many sacrifices, and I make them still, but I've not been treated well."

Left alone in the dusky little sitting-room, Robert Audley folded his arms, and sat absently staring at the floor.

George was gone, then; he might receive some

letter of explanation, perhaps, when he returned
to London; but the chances were that he would
never see his old friend again.

"And to think that I should care so much for
the fellow!" he said, lifting his eyebrows to the
centre of his forehead.

"The place smells of stale tobacco like a tap-
room," he muttered presently; "there can be no
harm in my smoking a cigar here."

He took one from the case in his pocket; there
was a spark of fire in the little grate, and he
looked about for something to light his cigar
with.

A twisted piece of paper lay half burned upon
the hearthrug; he picked it up, and unfolded it,
in order to get a better pipe-light by folding it the
other way of the paper. As he did so, absently
glancing at the pencilled writing upon the fragment of thin paper, a portion of a name caught
his eye—a portion of the name that was most in
his thoughts. He took the scrap of paper to
the window, and examined it by the declining
light.

It was part of a telegraphic despatch. The upper portion had been burnt away, but the more important part, the greater part of the message itself, remained.

alboys came to   last night, and left by the mail for London, on his way for Liverpool, whence he was to sail for Sydney.

The date and the name and address of the sender of the message had been burnt with the heading. Robert Audley's face blanched to a deathly whiteness. He carefully folded the scrap of paper, and placed it between the leaves of his pocket-book.

"My God !" he said, "what is the meaning of this ? I shall go to Liverpool to-night, and make inquiries there."

CHAPTER XIII.

TROUBLED DREAMS.

ROBERT AUDLEY left Southampton by the mail, and let himself into his chambers just as the dawn was creeping cold and grey into the solitary rooms, and the canaries were beginning to rustle their feathers feebly in the early morning.

There were several letters in the box behind the door, but there was none from George Talboys.

The young barrister was worn out by a long day spent in hurrying from place to place. The usual lazy monotony of his life had been broken as it had never been broken before in eight-and-twenty tranquil, easy-going years. His mind was beginning to grow confused upon the point of time. It seemed to him months since he had lost sight of George Talboys. It was so difficult to believe that it was less than forty-eight hours

ago that the young man had left him asleep under
the willows by the trout-stream.

His eyes were painfully weary for want of sleep.
He searched about the rooms for some time, looking in all sorts of impossible places for a letter
from George Talboys, and then threw himself
dressed upon his friend's bed, in the room with
the canaries and geraniums.

"I shall wait for to-morrow morning's post,"
he said, "and if that brings no letter from
George I shall start for Liverpool without a
moment's delay."

He was thoroughly exhausted, and fell into a
heavy sleep—a sleep which was profound without
being altogether refreshing, for he was tormented
all the time by disagreeable dreams — dreams
which were painful, not from any horror in themselves, but from a vague and wearying sense of
their confusion and absurdity.

At one time he was pursuing strange people
and entering strange houses in the endeavour to
unravel the mystery of the telegraphic despatch;
at another time he was in the churchyard at

Ventnor, gazing at the headstone George had ordered for the grave of his dead wife. Once in the long rambling mystery of these dreams he went to the grave, and found this headstone gone, and on remonstrating with the stonemason, was told that the man had a reason for removing the inscription, a reason that Robert would some day learn.

He started from his dreams to find there was some one knocking at the outer door of his chambers.

It was a dreary wet morning, the rain beating against the windows, and the canaries twittering dismally to each other—complaining, perhaps, of the bad weather. Robert could not tell how long the person had been knocking. He had heard the sound with his dreams, and when he woke he was only half conscious of outer things.

"It is that stupid Mrs. Maloney, I dare say," he muttered. "She may knock again for all I care. Why can't she use her duplicate key, instead of dragging a man out of bed when he's half dead with fatigue?"

The person, whoever it was, did knock again, and then desisted, apparently tired out ; but about a minute afterwards a key turned in the door.

" She had her key with her all the time, then," said Robert.   " I'm very glad I didn't get up."

The door between the sitting-room and bed-room was half open, and he could see the laundress bustling about, dusting the furniture, and re-arranging things that had never been disarranged.

"Is that you, Mrs. Maloney ? " he asked.

"Yes, Sir."

" Then why, in goodness' name, did you make that row at the door, when you had a key with you all the time ? "

" A row at the door, Sir ! "

"Yes ; that infernal knocking."

"Sure I never knocked, Misther Audley, but walked straight in with the key——"

"Then who did knock ?   There's been some one kicking up a row at that door for a quarter of an hour I should think ; you must have met him going down-stairs."

" But I'm rather late this morning, Sir, for I've

been in Mr. Martin's rooms first, and I've come straight from the floor above."

"Then you didn't see any one at the door, or on the stairs?"

"Not a mortal soul, Sir."

"Was ever anything so provoking?" said Robert. "To think that I should have let this person go away without ascertaining who he was, or what he wanted! How do I know that it was not some one with a message or a letter from George Talboys?"

"Sure, if it was, Sir, he'll come again," said Mrs. Maloney, soothingly.

"Yes, of course, if it was anything of consequence, he'll come again," muttered Robert. The fact was, that from the moment of finding the telegraphic message at Southampton all hope of hearing of George had faded out of his mind. He felt that there was some mystery involved in the disappearance of his friend—some treachery towards himself, or towards George. What if the young man's greedy old father-in-law had tried to separate them on account of the monetary trust

lodged in Robert Audley's hands? Or what if,
since even in these civilised days all kinds of
unsuspected horrors are constantly committed—
what if the old man had decoyed George down to
Southampton, and made away with him in order
to get possession of that £20,000, left in Robert's
custody for little Georgey's use?

But neither of these suppositions explained the
telegraphic message, and it was the telegraphic
message which had filled Robert's mind with a
vague sense of alarm.   The postman brought no
letter from George Talboys, and the person who
had knocked at the door of the chambers did not
return between seven and nine o'clock, so Robert
Audley left Fig-tree Court once more in search of
his friend.   This time he told the cabman to drive
to the Euston Station, and in twenty minutes he
was on the platform, making inquiries about the
trains.

The Liverpool express had started half an hour
before he reached the station, and he had to wait
an hour and a quarter for a slow train to take him
to his destination.

Robert Audley chafed cruelly at this delay. Half a dozen vessels might sail for Australia while he roamed up and down the long platform, tumbling over trucks and porters, and swearing at his ill-luck.

He bought the *Times* newspaper, and looked instinctively at the second column, with a morbid interest in the advertisements of people missing—sons, brothers, and husbands who had left their homes, never to return or to be heard of more.

There was one advertisement of a young man who was found drowned somewhere on the Lambeth shore.

What if that should have been George's fate? No; the telegraphic message involved his father-in-law in the fact of his disappearance, and every speculation about him must start from that one point.

It was eight o'clock in the evening when Robert got into Liverpool, too late for anything except to make inquiries as to what vessels had sailed within the last two days for the antipodes.

An emigrant ship had sailed at four o'clock

that afternoon—the Victoria Regia, bound for Melbourne.

The result of his inquiries amounted to this—if he wanted to find out who had sailed in the Victoria Regia, he must wait till the next morning, and apply for information of that vessel.

Robert Audley was at the office at nine o'clock the next morning, and was the first person after the clerks who entered it.

He met with every civility from the clerk to whom he applied. The young man referred to his books, and running his pen down the list of passengers who had sailed in the Victoria Regia, told Robert that there was no one amongst them of the name of Talboys. He pushed his inquiries further. Had any of the passengers entered their names within a short time of the vessel's sailing?

One of the other clerks looked up from his desk as Robert asked this question. Yes, he said, he remembered a young man's coming into the office at half-past three o'clock in the afternoon, and paying his passage-money. His name was the last on the list—Thomas Brown.

Robert Audley shrugged his shoulders. There could have been no possible reason for George's taking a feigned name. He asked the clerk who had last spoken if he could remember the appearance of this Mr. Thomas Brown.

No, the office was crowded at the time; people were running in and out, and he had not taken any particular notice of this last passenger.

Robert thanked them for their civility, and wished them good morning. As he was leaving the office one of the young men called after him.

"Oh, by the bye, Sir," he said, "I remember one thing about this Mr. Thomas Brown—his arm was in a sling."

There was nothing more for Robert Audley to do but to return to town. He re-entered his chambers at six o'clock that evening, thoroughly worn out once more with his useless search.

Mrs. Maloney brought him his dinner and a pint of wine from a tavern in the Strand. The evening was raw and chilly, and the laundress had lighted a good fire in the sitting-room grate.

After eating about half a mutton chop, Robert

sat with his wine untasted upon the table before him, smoking cigars and staring into the blaze.

"George Talboys never sailed for Australia," he said, after long and painful reflection. "If he is alive he is still in England, and if he is dead his body is hidden in some corner of England."

He sat for hours smoking and thinking—troubled and gloomy thoughts, leaving a dark shadow upon his moody face, which neither the brilliant light of the gas nor the red blaze of the fire could dispel.

Very late in the evening he rose from his chair, pushed away the table, wheeled his desk over to the fire-place, took out a sheet of foolscap, and dipped a pen in the ink.

But after doing this he paused, leaned his forehead upon his hand, and once more relapsed into thought.

"I shall draw up a record of all that has occurred between our going down to Essex and to-night, beginning at the very beginning."

He drew up this record in short detached sentences, which he numbered as he wrote.

It ran thus :—

"JOURNAL OF FACTS CONNECTED WITH THE DISAPPEARANCE
OF GEORGE TALBOYS, INCLUSIVE OF FACTS WHICH HAVE
NO APPARENT RELATION TO THAT CIRCUMSTANCE."

In spite of the troubled state of his mind he was rather inclined to be proud of the official appearance of this heading. He sat for some time looking at it with affection, and with the feather of his pen in his mouth. "Upon my word," he said, "I begin to think that I ought to have pursued my profession, instead of dawdling my life away as I have done."

He smoked half a cigar before he had got his thoughts in proper train, and then began to write :—

"1. I write to Alicia, proposing to take George down to the Court.

"2. Alicia writes, objecting to the visit on the part of Lady Audley.

"3. We go to Essex in spite of this objection. I see my lady. My lady refuses to be introduced to George that particular evening on the score of fatigue.

"4. Sir Michael invites George and me to dinner for the following evening.

"5. My lady receives a telegraphic despatch the next morning which summons her to London.

"6. Alicia shows me a letter from my lady, in which she requests to be told when I and my friend, Mr. Talboys, mean to leave Essex. To this letter is subjoined a postscript reiterating the above request.

"7. We call at the Court, and ask to see the house. My lady's apartments are locked.

"8. We get at the aforesaid apartments by means of a secret passage, the existence of which is unknown to my lady. In one of the rooms we find her portrait.

"9. George is frightened at the storm. His conduct is exceedingly strange for the rest of the evening.

"10. George quite himself again the following morning. I propose leaving Audley Court immediately; he prefers remaining till the evening.

"11. We go out fishing. George leaves me to go to the Court.

"12. The last positive information I can obtain of him in Essex is at the Court, where the servant says he thinks Mr. Talboys told him he would go and look for my lady in the grounds.

"13. I receive information about him at the station which may, or may not, be correct.

"14. I hear of him positively once more at Southampton, where, according to his father-in-law, he had been for an hour on the previous night.

"15. The telegraphic message."

When Robert Audley had completed this brief record, which he drew up with great deliberation, and with frequent pauses for reflection, alterations, and erasures, he sat for a long time contemplating the written page.

At last he read it carefully over, stopping at some of the numbered paragraphs, and marking several of them with a pencilled cross; then he folded the sheet of foolscap, went over to a cabinet on the opposite side of the room, unlocked it, and placed the paper in that very pigeon-hole into which he had thrust Alicia's letter—the pigeon-hole marked *Important*.

Having done this, he returned to his easy chair by the fire, pushed away his desk, and lighted a cigar. "It's as dark as midnight from first to last," he said; "and the clue to the mystery must be found either at Southampton or in Essex. Be it how it may, my mind is made up. I shall first go to Audley Court, and look for George Talboys in a narrow radius."

CHAPTER XIV.

PHŒBE'S SUITOR.

" Mr. George Talboys.—Any person who has met this gentleman since the 7th inst., or who possesses any information respecting him subsequent to that date, will be liberally rewarded on communicating with A. Z., 14, Chancery Lane."

Sir Michael Audley read the above advertisement in the second column of the *Times*, as he sat at breakfast with my lady and Alicia two or three days after Robert's return to town.

" Robert's friend has not yet been heard of, then," said the baronet, after reading the advertisement to his wife and daughter.

" As for that," replied my lady, " I cannot help wondering who can be silly enough to advertise for him. The young man was evidently of a restless, roving disposition—a sort of Bamfylde

Moore Carew of modern life, whom no attraction
could ever keep in one spot."

Though the advertisement appeared three suc-
cessive times, the party at the Court attached
very little importance to Mr. Talboys' disappearance; and after this one occasion his name was
never again mentioned by either Sir Michael, my
lady, or Alicia.

Alicia Audley and her pretty stepmother were
by no means any better friends after that quiet
evening on which the young barrister had dined
at the Court.

"She is a vain, frivolous, heartless little
coquette," said Alicia, addressing herself to her
Newfoundland dog, Cæsar, who was the sole
recipient of the young lady's confidences; "she
is a practised and consummate flirt, Cæsar; and
not contented with setting her yellow ringlets
and her silly giggle at half the men in Essex, she
must needs make that stupid cousin of mine
dance attendance upon her. I haven't common
patience with her."

In proof of which last assertion Miss Alicia

Audley treated her stepmother with such very palpable impertinence that Sir Michael felt himself called upon to remonstrate with his only daughter.

"The poor little woman is very sensitive, you know, Alicia," the baronet said gravely, "and she feels your conduct most acutely."

"I don't believe it a bit, papa," answered Alicia stoutly. "You think her sensitive because she has soft little white hands, and big blue eyes with long lashes, and all manner of affected, fantastical ways, which you stupid men call fascinating. Sensitive! Why, I've seen her do cruel things with those slender white fingers, and laugh at the pain she inflicted. I'm very sorry, papa," she added, softened a little by her father's look of distress; "though she has come between us, and robbed poor Alicia of the love of that dear, generous heart, I wish I could like her for your sake; but I can't, I can't, and no more can Cæsar. She came up to him once with her red lips apart, and her little white teeth glistening between them, and stroked his great head with her soft hand;

but if I had not had hold of his collar, he would have flown at her throat and strangled her. She may bewitch every man in Essex, but she'd never make friends with my dog."

"Your dog shall be shot," answered Sir Michael angrily, "if his vicious temper ever endangers Lucy."

The Newfoundland rolled his eyes slowly round in the direction of the speaker, as if he understood every word that had been said. Lady Audley happened to enter the room at this very moment, and the animal cowered down by the side of his mistress with a suppressed growl. There was something in the manner of the dog which was, if anything, more indicative of terror than of fury, incredible as it appears that Cæsar should be frightened of so fragile a creature as Lucy Audley.

Amiable as was my lady's nature, she could not live long at the Court without discovering Alicia's dislike to her. She never alluded to it but once; then, shrugging her graceful white shoulders, she said with a sigh:

"It seems very hard that you cannot love me, Alicia, for I have never been used to make enemies; but since it seems that it must be so, I cannot help it. If we cannot be friends, let us at least be neutral. You won't try to injure me?"

"Injure you!" exclaimed Alicia; "how should I injure you?"

"You'll not try to deprive me of your father's affection?"

"I may not be as amiable as you are, my lady, and I may not have the same sweet smiles and pretty words for every stranger I meet, but I am not capable of a contemptible meanness; and even if I were, I think you are so secure of my father's love, that nothing but your own act will ever deprive you of it."

"What a severe creature you are, Alicia!" said my lady, making a little grimace. "I suppose you mean to infer by all that, that I'm deceitful. Why, I can't help smiling at people, and speaking prettily to them. I know I'm no *better* than the rest of the world, but I can't help it if I'm *pleasanter*. It's constitutional."

Alicia having thus entirely shut the door upon
all intimacy between Lady Audley and herself,
and Sir Michael being chiefly occupied in agri-
cultural pursuits and manly sports, which kept
him away from home, it was, perhaps, only natural
that my lady, being of an eminently social disposition, should find herself thrown a good deal
upon her white-eyelashed maid for society.

Phœbe Marks was exactly the sort of girl who
is generally promoted from the post of lady's-
maid to that of companion. She had just sufficient education to enable her to understand her
mistress when Lucy chose to allow herself to run
riot in a species of intellectual tarantella, in
which her tongue went mad to the sound of its
own rattle, as the Spanish dancer at the noise of
his castanets. Phœbe knew enough of the French
language to be able to dip into the yellow-paper-
covered novels which my lady ordered from the
Burlington Arcade, and to discourse with her
mistress upon the questionable subjects of those
romances. The likeness which the lady's-maid
bore to Lucy Audley was, perhaps, a point of

sympathy between the two women. It was not
to be called a striking likeness ; a stranger might
have seen them both together, and yet have failed
to remark it. But there were certain dim and
shadowy lights in which, meeting Phœbe Marks
gliding softly through the dark oak passages of
the Court, or under the shrouded avenues in the
garden, you might have easily mistaken her for
my lady.

Sharp October winds were sweeping the leaves
from the limes in the long avenue, and driving
them in withered heaps with a ghostly rustling
noise along the dry gravel walks. The old well
must have been half choked up with the leaves
that drifted about it, and whirled in eddying
circles into its black, broken mouth. On the still
bosom of the fish-pond the same withered leaves
slowly rotted away, mixing themselves with the
tangled weeds that discoloured the surface of
the water. All the gardeners Sir Michael could
employ could not keep the impress of autumn's
destroying hand from the grounds about the
Court.

"How I hate this desolate month!" my lady
said, as she walked about the garden, shivering
beneath her sable mantle. "Everything dropping to ruin and decay, and the cold flicker of the
sun lighting up the ugliness of the earth, as the
glare of gas-lamps lights the wrinkles of an old
woman. Shall I ever grow old, Phœbe? Will
my hair ever drop off as the leaves are falling from
those trees, and leave me wan and bare like them?
What is to become of me when I grow old?"

She shivered at the thought of this more than
she had done at the cold wintry breeze, and
muffling herself closely in her fur, walked so fast,
that her maid had some difficulty in keeping up
with her.

"Do you remember, Phœbe," she said presently, relaxing her pace, "do you remember
that French story we read—the story of a beautiful woman who committed some crime—I forget
what—in the zenith of her power and loveliness,
when all Paris drank to her every night, and
when the people ran away from the carriage of
the king to flock about hers, and get a peep at

her face? Do you remember how she kept the secret of what she had done for nearly half a century, spending her old age in her family château, beloved and honoured by all the province, as an uncanonised saint and benefactress to the poor; and how, when her hair was white, and her eyes almost blind with age, the secret was revealed through one of those strange accidents by which such secrets always are revealed in romances, and she was tried, found guilty, and condemned to be burned alive? The king who had worn her colours was dead and gone; the court of which she had been the star had passed away; powerful functionaries and great magistrates, who might perhaps have helped her, were mouldering in their graves; brave young cavaliers, who would have died for her, had fallen upon distant battle-fields; she had lived to see the age to which she had belonged fade like a dream; and she went to the stake, followed only by a few ignorant country people, who forgot all her bounties, and hooted at her for a wicked sorceress."

"I don't care for such dismal stories, my lady,"

said Phœbe Marks with a shudder. "One has no need to read books to give one the horrors in this dull place."

Lady Audley shrugged her shoulders and laughed at her maid's candour.

"It is a dull place, Phœbe," she said, "though it doesn't do to say so to my dear old husband. Though I am the wife of one of the most influential men in the county, I don't know that I wasn't nearly as well off at Mr. Dawson's; and yet it's something to wear sables that cost sixty guineas, and have a thousand pounds spent on the decorations of one's apartments."

Treated as a companion by her mistress, in the receipt of the most liberal wages, and with perquisites such as perhaps no lady's-maid ever had before, it was strange that Phœbe Marks should wish to leave her situation; but it was not the less a fact that she was anxious to exchange all the advantages of Audley Court for the very unpromising prospect which awaited her as the wife of her cousin Luke.

The young man had contrived in some manner

to associate himself with the improved fortunes
of his sweetheart. He had never allowed Phœbe
any peace till she obtained for him, by the aid of
my lady's interference, a situation as under-groom
at the Court.

He never rode out with either Alicia or Sir
Michael; but on one of the few occasions upon
which my lady mounted the pretty little grey
thoroughbred reserved for her use, he contrived to
attend her in her ride. He saw enough, in the
very first half hour they were out, to discover
that, graceful as Lucy Audley might look in her
long blue cloth habit, she was a timid horsewoman, and utterly unable to manage the animal
she rode.

Lady Audley remonstrated with her maid
upon her folly in wishing to marry the uncouth
groom.

The two women were seated together over the
fire in my lady's dressing-room, the grey sky
closing in upon the October afternoon, and the
black tracery of ivy darkening the casement
windows.

"You surely are not in love with the awkward, ugly creature, are you, Phœbe?" asked my lady sharply.

The girl was sitting on a low stool at her mistress's feet. She did not answer my lady's question immediately, but sat for some time looking vacantly into the red abyss in the hollow fire.

Presently she said, rather as if she had been thinking aloud than answering Lucy's question—

"I don't think I can love him. We have been together from children, and I promised, when I was little better than fifteen, that I'd be his wife. I daren't break that promise now. There have been times when I've made up the very sentence I meant to say to him, telling him that I couldn't keep my faith with him; but the words have died upon my lips, and I've sat looking at him, with a choking sensation in my throat that wouldn't let me speak. I daren't refuse to marry him. I've often watched and watched him, as he has sat slicing away at a hedge-stake with his great clasp-knife, till I have thought that it is just such men as he who have decoyed their sweethearts into

lonely places, and murdered them for being false
to their word. When he was a boy he was always
violent and revengeful. I saw him once take up
that very knife in a quarrel with his mother. I
tell you, my lady, I must marry him."

"You silly girl, you shall do nothing of the
kind!" answered Lucy. "You think he'll
murder you, do you? Do you think, then, if
murder is in him, you would be any safer as his
wife? If you thwarted him, or made him jealous;
if he wanted to marry another woman, or to get
hold of some poor, pitiful bit of money of yours,
couldn't he murder you then? I tell you you
shan't marry him, Phœbe. In the first place, I
hate the man; and, in the next place, I can't
afford to part with you. We'll give him a few
pounds and send him about his business."

Phœbe Marks caught my lady's hands in hers,
and clasped them convulsively.

"My lady—my good, kind mistress!" she
cried vehemently, "don't try to thwart me in
this—don't ask me to thwart him. I tell you I
must marry him. You don't know what he is.

It will be my ruin, and the ruin of others, if I break my word. I must marry him!"

"Very well, then, Phœbe," answered her mistress, "I can't oppose you. There must be some secret at the bottom of all this."

"There is, my lady," said the girl, with her face turned away from Lucy.

"I shall be very sorry to lose you; but I have promised to stand your friend in all things. What does your cousin mean to do for a living when you are married?"

"He would like to take a public-house."

"Then he shall take a public-house, and the sooner he drinks himself to death the better. Sir Michael dines at a bachelor's party at Major Margrave's this evening, and my step-daughter is away with her friends at the Grange. You can bring your cousin into the drawing-room after dinner, and I'll tell him what I mean to do for him."

"You are very good, my lady," Phœbe answered with a sigh.

Lady Audley sat in the glow of firelight and wax candles in the luxurious drawing-room; the amber damask cushions of the sofa contrasting with her dark violet velvet dress, and her rippling hair falling about her neck in a golden haze. Everywhere around her were the evidences of wealth and splendour; while in strange contrast to all this, and to her own beauty, the awkward groom stood rubbing his bullet head as my lady explained to him what she meant to do for her confidential maid. Lucy's promises were very liberal, and she had expected that, uncouth as the man was, he would in his own rough manner have expressed his gratitude.

To her surprise he stood staring at the floor without uttering a word in answer to her offer. Phœbe was standing close to his elbow, and seemed distressed at the man's rudeness.

"Tell my lady how thankful you are, Luke," she said.

"But I'm not so over and above thankful," answered her lover savagely. "Fifty pound ain't much to start a public. You'll make it a hundred, my lady."

"I shall do nothing of the kind," said Lady

Audley, her clear blue eyes flashing with indignation, " and I wonder at your impertinence in asking it."

"Oh yes, you will though," answered Luke,
with quiet insolence, that had a hidden meaning.
" You'll make it a hundred, my lady."

Lady Audley rose from her seat, looked the
man steadfastly in the face till his determined
gaze sank under hers; then walking straight up
to her maid, she said in a high, piercing voice,
peculiar to her in moments of intense agitation,
" Phœbe Marks, you have told *this man !* "

The girl fell on her knees at my lady's feet.

" Oh, forgive me, forgive me ! " she cried.
" He forced it from me, or I would never, never
have told ! "

CHAPTER XV.

ON THE WATCH.

Upon a lowering morning late in November, with the yellow fog low upon the flat meadows, and the blinded cattle groping their way through the dim obscurity, and blundering stupidly against black and leafless hedges, or stumbling into ditches, undistinguishable in the hazy atmosphere; with the village church looming brown and dingy through the uncertain light; with every winding path and cottage door, every gable-end and grey old chimney, every village child and straggling cur, seeming strange and weird of aspect in the semi-darkness, Phœbe Marks and her cousin Luke made their way through the churchyard of Audley, and presented themselves before a shivering curate, whose surplice hung in damp folds, soddened by the morning mist, and whose temper was not improved by

his having waited five minutes for the bride and
bridegroom.

Luke Marks, dressed in his ill-fitting Sunday
clothes, looked by no means handsomer than in
his every-day apparel; but Phœbe, arrayed in a
rustling silk of delicate grey, that had been worn
about half a dozen times by her mistress, looked,
as the few spectators of the ceremony remarked,
quite the lady.

A very dim and shadowy lady; vague of out-
line, and faint of colouring; with eyes, hair,
complexion, and dress all melting into such pale
and uncertain shades that, in the obscure light
of the foggy November morning, a superstitious
stranger might have mistaken the bride for the
ghost of some other bride, dead and buried in the
vaults below the church.

Mr. Luke Marks, the hero of the occasion,
thought very little of all this. He had secured
the wife of his choice, and the object of his life-
long ambition—a public-house. My lady had
provided the seventy-five pounds necessary for
the purchase of the good-will and fixtures, with

the stock of ales and spirits, of a small inn in the centre of a lonely little village, perched on the summit of a hill, and called Mount Stanning. It was not a very pretty house to look at; it had something of a tumble-down, weather-beaten appearance, standing as it did upon high ground, sheltered only by four or five bare and overgrown poplars, that had shot up too rapidly. for their strength, and had a blighted forlorn look in consequence. The wind had had its own way with the Castle Inn, and had sometimes made cruel use of its power. It was the wind that battered and bent the low, thatched roofs of out-houses and stables, till they hung over and lurched forward, as a slouched hat hangs over the low forehead of some village ruffian; it was the wind that shook and rattled the wooden shutters before the narrow casements, till they hung broken and dilapidated upon their rusty hinges; it was the wind that overthrew the pigeon-house, and broke the vane that had been impudently set up to tell the movements of its mightiness; it was the wind that made light of

any little bit of wooden trellis-work, or creeping
plant, or tiny balcony, or any modest decoration
whatsoever, and tore and scattered it in its scornful fury; it was the wind that left mossy secre-
tions on the discoloured surface of the plaster
walls; it was the wind, in short, that shattered,
and ruined, and rent, and trampled upon the
tottering pile of buildings, and then flew shriek-
ing off, to riot and glory in its destroying
strength. The dispirited proprietor grew tired
of his long struggle with this mighty enemy; so
the wind was left to work its own will, and the
Castle Inn fell slowly to decay. But for all that
it suffered without, it was not the less prosperous
within doors. Sturdy drovers stopped to drink
at the little bar; well-to-do farmers spent their
evenings and talked politics in the low, wain-
scoted parlour, while their horses munched some
suspicious mixture of mouldy hay and tolerable
beans in the tumble-down stables. Sometimes
even the members of the Audley hunt stopped to
drink and bait their horses at the Castle Inn;
while, on one grand and never-to-be-forgotten

occasion, a dinner had been ordered by the master of the hounds for some thirty gentlemen, and the proprietor driven nearly mad by the importance of the demand.

So Luke Marks, who was by no means troubled with an eye for the beautiful, thought himself very fortunate in becoming landlord of the Castle Inn, Mount Stanning.

A chaise-cart was waiting in the fog to convey the bride and bridegroom to their new home; and a few of the simple villagers, who had known Phœbe from a child, were lingering round the churchyard gate to bid her good-by. Her pale eyes were still paler from the tears she had shed, and the red rims which surrounded them. The bridegroom was annoyed at this exhibition of emotion.

"What are you blubbering for, lass?" he said fiercely. "If you didn't want to marry me, you should have told me so. I ain't going to murder you, am I?"

The lady's-maid shivered as he spoke to her, and dragged her little silk mantle closely round her.

"You're cold in all this here finery," said
Luke, staring at her costly dress with no expression of good-will. "Why can't women dress
according to their station? You won't have no
silk gowns out of my pocket, I can tell you."

He lifted the shivering girl into the chaise,
wrapped a rough great-coat about her, and drove
off through the yellow fog, followed by a feeble
cheer from two or three urchins clustered round
the gate.

A new maid was brought from London to
replace Phœbe Marks about the person of my
lady—a very showy damsel, who wore a black
satin gown, and rose-coloured ribbons in her cap,
and complained bitterly of the dulness of Audley
Court.

But Christmas brought visitors to the rambling
old mansion. A country squire and his fat wife
occupied the tapestried chamber; merry girls
scampered up and down the long passages, and
young men stared out of the latticed windows
watching for southerly winds and cloudy skies;
there was not an empty stall in the roomy old

stables; an extempore forge had been set up in
the yard for the shoeing of hunters; yelping dogs
made the place noisy with their perpetual clamour;
strange servants horded together on the garret
storey; and every little casement hidden away
under some pointed gable, and every dormer window in the quaint old roof, glimmered upon the
winter's night with its separate taper, till, coming
suddenly upon Audley Court, the benighted
stranger, misled by the light and noise, and
bustle of the place, might have easily fallen into
young Marlowe's error, and have mistaken the
hospitable mansion for a good, old-fashioned inn,
such as have faded from this earth since the last
mail coach and prancing tits took their last melancholy journey to the knacker's yard.

Amongst other visitors Mr. Robert Audley
came down to Essex for the hunting season, with
half-a-dozen French novels, a case of cigars, and
three pounds of Turkish tobacco in his portmanteau.

The honest young country squires, who talked
all breakfast time of Flying Dutchman fillies and

Voltigeur colts; of glorious runs of seven hours'
hard riding over three counties, and a midnight
homeward ride of thirty miles upon their covert
hacks; and who ran away from the well-spread
table with their mouths full of cold sirloin to
look at that off pastern, or that sprained fore-arm,
or the colt that had just come back from the
veterinary surgeon's, set down Mr. Robert Audley,
dawdling over a slice of bread and marmalade, as
a person utterly unworthy of any remark whatsoever.

The young barrister had brought a couple of
dogs with him; and the country gentleman who
gave fifty pounds for a pointer, and travelled a
couple of hundred miles to look at a leash of
setters before he struck a bargain, laughed aloud
at the two miserable curs; one of which had
followed Robert Audley through Chancery Lane
and half the length of Holborn; while his companion had been taken by the barrister *vi et
armis* from a costermonger who was ill-using him.
And as Robert furthermore insisted on having
these two deplorable animals under his easy-chair

in the drawing-room, much to the annoyance of my lady, who, as we know, hated all dogs, the visitors at Audley Court looked upon the baronet's nephew as an inoffensive species of maniac.

During other visits to the Court, Robert Audley had made a feeble show of joining in the sports of the merry assembly. He had jogged across half a dozen ploughed fields on a quiet grey pony of Sir Michael's, and drawing up breathless and panting at the door of some farm-house, had expressed his intention of following the hounds no further *that* morning. He had even gone so far as to put on, with great labour, a pair of skates, with a view to taking a turn on the frozen surface of the fish-pond, and had fallen ignominiously at the first attempt, lying placidly extended on the flat of his back until such time as the bystanders should think fit to pick him up. He had occupied the back seat in a dog-cart during a pleasant morning drive, vehemently protesting against being taken up-hill, and requiring the vehicle to be stopped every ten minutes for the re-adjustment of the cushions. But this year

he showed no inclination for any of these out-
door amusements. He spent his time entirely in
lounging in the drawing-room, and making himself agreeable, after his own lazy fashion, to my
lady and Alicia.

Lady Audley received her nephew's attentions
in that graceful, half-childish fashion which her
admirers found so charming; but Alicia was
indignant at the change in her cousin's conduct.

"You were always a poor, spiritless fellow,
Bob," said the young lady, contemptuously, as
she bounced into the drawing-room, in her riding
habit, after a hunting breakfast, from which
Robert had absented himself, preferring a cup of
tea in my lady's boudoir; "but this year I don't
know what has come to you. You are good for
nothing but to hold a skein of silk or read Tenny-
son to Lady Audley."

"My dear, hasty, impetuous Alicia, don't be
violent," said the young man imploringly. "A
conclusion isn't a five-barred gate; and you
needn't give your judgment its head, as you give

your mare, Atalanta, hers, when you're flying across country at the heels of an unfortunate fox. Lady Audley interests me, and my uncle's county friends do not. Is that a sufficient answer, Alicia?"

Miss Audley gave her head a little scornful toss.

"It's as good an answer as I shall ever get from you, Bob," she said impatiently; "but pray amuse yourself in your own way; loll in an easy-chair all day, with those two absurd dogs asleep on your knees; spoil my lady's window-curtains with your cigars; and annoy everybody in the house with your stupid, inanimate countenance."

Mr. Robert Audley opened his handsome grey eyes to their widest extent at this tirade, and looked helplessly at Miss Alicia.

The young lady was walking up and down the room, slashing the skirt of her habit with her riding-whip. Her eyes sparkled with an angry flash, and a crimson glow burned under her clear brown skin. The young barrister knew very well by these diagnostics, that his cousin was in a passion.

"Yes," she repeated, "your stupid, inanimate countenance. Do you know, Robert Audley, that with all your mock amiability, you are brimful of conceit and superciliousness. You look down upon our amusements; you lift up your eyebrows, and shrug your shoulders, and throw yourself back in your chair, and wash your hands of us and our pleasures. You are a selfish, cold-hearted Sybarite——"

"Alicia! Good—gracious—me!"

The morning paper dropped out of his hands, and he sat feebly staring at his assailant.

"Yes, *selfish*, Robert Audley! You take home half-starved dogs, because you like half-starved dogs. You stoop down and pat the head of every good-for-nothing cur in the village street, because you like good-for-nothing curs. You notice little children, and give them halfpence, because it pleases you to do so. But you lift your eyebrows a quarter of a yard when poor Sir Harry Towers tells a stupid story, and stare the poor fellow out of countenance with your lazy insolence. As to your amiability, you would let a man hit you, and say 'Thank you' for the blow, rather than take the trouble to hit him again; but you wouldn't go half a mile out of your way to serve your dearest friend. Sir Harry is worth twenty of you, though he *did* write to ask if my ma-a-i-r, Atalanta, had recovered from the sprain. He can't spell, or lift his eyebrows to the roots of his hair; but he would go through fire and water for the girl he loves; while *you*—"

At this very point, when Robert was most prepared to encounter his cousin's violence, and when Miss Alicia seemed about to make her strongest attack, the young lady broke down altogether and burst into tears.

Robert sprang from his easy-chair, upsetting his dogs on the carpet.

" Alicia, my darling, what is it ?"

" It's—it's—it's the feather of my hat that got into my eyes," sobbed his cousin; and before Robert could investigate the truth of this assertion Alicia had darted out of the room.

Mr. Audley was preparing to follow her, when he heard her voice in the courtyard below, amidst the trampling of horses and the clamour of visitors, dogs, and grooms. Sir Harry Towers, the most aristocratic young sportsman in the neighbourhood, had just taken her little foot in his hand as she sprang into her saddle.

"Good heavens!" exclaimed Robert, as he watched the merry party of equestrians until they disappeared under the archway. "What does all this mean? How charmingly she sits her horse! What a pretty figure, too, and a fine, candid, brown, rosy face; but to fly at a fellow like that, without the least provocation! That's the consequence of letting a girl follow the hounds. She learns to look at everything in life as she does at six feet of timber or a sunk fence; she goes through the world as she goes across country—straight ahead, and over everything. Such a nice girl as she might have been, too, if she'd been brought up in Fig-tree Court! If ever I marry, and have daughters (which remote contingency may Heaven forefend!), they shall be educated in Paper Buildings, take their sole exercise in the Temple Gardens, and they shall never go beyond the gates till they are marriageable, when I will take them straight across Fleet Street to St. Dunstan's Church, and deliver them into the hands of their husbands."

With such reflections as these did Mr. Robert Audley beguile the time until my lady re-entered the drawing-room, fresh and radiant in her elegant morning costume, her yellow curls glistening with the perfumed waters in which she had bathed, and her velvet-covered sketch-book in her arms. She planted a little easel upon a table by the window, seated herself before it, and began to mix the colours upon her palette, Robert watching her out of his half-closed eyes.

"You are sure my cigar does not annoy you, Lady Audley?"

"Oh no, indeed; I am quite used to the smell of tobacco. Mr. Dawson, the surgeon, smoked all the evening, when I lived in his house."

"Dawson is a good fellow, isn't he?" Robert asked carelessly.

My lady burst into her pretty gushing laugh.

"The dearest of good creatures," she said. "He paid me five-and-twenty pounds a year— only fancy—that made six pounds five a quarter. How well I remember receiving the money—six dingy old sovereigns, and a little heap of untidy, dirty silver, that came straight from the till in the surgery! And then how glad I was to get it; while *now*—I can't help laughing while I think of it—these colours I am using cost a guinea each at Winsor and Newton's—the carmine and ultramarine thirty shillings. I gave Mrs. Dawson one of my silk dresses the other day, and the poor thing kissed me, and the surgeon carried the bundle home under his cloak."

My lady laughed long and joyously at the thought. Her colours were mixed; she was copying a water-coloured sketch of an impossibly beautiful Italian peasant, in an impossibly

Turneresque atmosphere. The sketch was nearly finished, and she had only to put in some critical little touches with the most delicate of her sable pencils. She prepared herself daintily for the work, looking sideways at the painting.

All this time Mr. Robert Audley's eyes were fixed intently on her pretty face.

"It *is* a change," he said, after so long a pause that my lady might have forgotten what she had been talking of; "it *is* a change! Some women would do a great deal to accomplish such a change as that."

Lucy Audley's clear blue eyes dilated as she fixed them suddenly on the young barrister. The winter sunlight, gleaming full upon her face from a side window, lit up the azure of those beautiful eyes, till their colour seemed to flicker and tremble betwixt blue and green, as the opal tints of the sea change upon a summer's day. The small brush fell from her hand, and blotted out the peasant's face under a widening circle of crimson lake.

Robert Audley was tenderly coaxing the crumpled leaf of his cigar with cautious fingers.

"My friend at the corner of Chancery Lane has not given me such good Manillas as usual," he murmured. "If ever you smoke, my dear aunt (and I am told that many women take a quiet weed under the rose), be very careful how you choose your cigars."

My lady drew a long breath, picked up her brush, and laughed aloud at Robert's advice.

"What an eccentric creature you are, Mr. Audley ! Do you know that you sometimes puzzle me——"

"Not more than you puzzle me, my dear aunt."

My lady put away her colours and sketch-book, and seating herself in the deep recess of another window at a considerable distance from Robert Audley, settled herself to a large piece of Berlin-wool work—a piece of embroidery which the Penelopes of ten or twelve years ago were very fond of exercising their ingenuity upon—the Olden Time at Bolton Abbey.

Seated in the embrasure of this window, my
lady was separated from Robert Audley by the
whole length of the room, and the young man
could only catch an occasional glimpse of her
fair face, surrounded by its bright aureole of
hazy golden hair.

Robert Audley had been a week at the Court,
but as yet neither he nor my lady had mentioned
the name of George Talboys.

This morning, however, after exhausting the
usual topics of conversation, Lady Audley made
an inquiry about her nephew's friend—" that
Mr. George—George——" she said, hesitating.

" Talboys," suggested Robert.

" Yes, to be sure — Mr. George Talboys.
Rather a singular name by-the-bye, and certainly,
by all accounts, a very singular person. Have
you seen him lately ? "

" I have not seen him since the 7th of
September—the day upon which he left me
asleep in the meadows on the other side of the
village."

" Dear me ! " exclaimed my lady, " what a

strange young man this Mr. George Talboys must be! Pray tell me all about it."

Robert told, in a few words, of his visit to Southampton, and his journey to Liverpool, with their different results, my lady listening very attentively.

In order to tell this story to better advantage the young man left his chair, and crossing the room, took up his place opposite to Lady Audley in the embrasure of the window.

" And what do you infer from all this ? " asked my lady after a pause.

" It is so great a mystery to me," he answered, " that I scarcely dare to draw any conclusion whatever; but in the obscurity I think I can grope my way to two suppositions, which to me seem almost certainties."

" And they are——"

" First, that George Talboys never went beyond Southampton. Secondly, that he never went to Southampton at all."

" But you traced him there. His father-in-law had seen him."

" I have reason to doubt his father-in-law's integrity."

" Good gracious me ! " cried my lady, piteously. " What do you mean by all this ? "

" Lady Audley," answered the young man gravely, " I have never practised as a barrister. I have enrolled myself in the ranks of a profession, the members of which hold solemn responsibilities, and have sacred duties to perform; and I have shrunk from those responsibilities and duties, as I have from all the fatigues of this troublesome life: but we are sometimes forced into the very position we have most avoided, and I have found myself lately compelled to think of these things. Lady Audley, did you ever study the theory of circumstantial evidence ? "

" How can you ask a poor little woman about such horrid things ? " exclaimed my lady.

" Circumstantial evidence," continued the young man, as if he scarcely heard Lady Audley's interruption, " that wonderful fabric which is built out of straws collected at every point of the compass, and which is yet strong enough to hang a man. Upon what infinitesimal trifles may sometimes hang the whole secret of some wicked mystery, inexplicable heretofore to the wisest upon the earth! A scrap of paper; a shred of some torn garment; the button off a coat; a word dropped incautiously from the over-cautious lips of guilt; the fragment of a letter; the shutting or opening of a door; a shadow on a window-blind; the accuracy of a moment; a thousand circumstances so slight as to be forgotten by the criminal, but links of steel in the wonderful chain forged by the science of the detective officer; and lo! the gallows is built up; the solemn bell tolls through the dismal grey of the early morning; the drop creaks under the guilty feet; and the penalty of crime is paid."

Faint shadows of green and crimson fell upon my lady's face from the painted escutcheons in the mullioned window by which she sat; but every trace of the natural colour of that face had faded out, leaving it a ghastly ashen grey.

Sitting quietly in her chair, her head fallen back upon the amber damask cushions, and her little hands lying powerless in her lap, Lady Audley had fainted away.

"The radius grows narrower day by day," said Robert Audley. "George Talboys never reached Southampton."

CHAPTER XVI.

ROBERT AUDLEY GETS HIS CONGÉ.

THE Christmas week was over, and one by one
the country visitors dropped away from Audley
Court.   The fat squire and his wife abandoned
the grey, tapestried chamber, and left the black-
browed warriors looming from the wall to scowl
upon and threaten new guests, or to glare venge-
fully upon vacancy.   The merry girls on the
second storey packed, or caused to be packed,
their trunks and imperials, and tumbled gauze
ball-dresses were taken home that had been
brought fresh to Audley.   Blundering old family
chariots, with horses whose untrimmed fetlocks
told of rougher work than even country roads,
were brought round to the broad space before
the grim oak door, and laden with chaotic heaps
of womanly luggage.   Pretty rosy faces peeped
out of the carriage windows to smile the last

farewell upon the group at the hall door, as the vehicle rattled and rumbled under the ivied archway.   Sir Michael was in request everywhere. Shaking hands with the young sportsmen; kissing the rosy-cheeked girls; sometimes even embracing portly matrons who came to thank him for their pleasant visit; everywhere genial, hospitable, generous, happy, and beloved, the baronet hurried from room to room, from the hall to the stables, from the stables to the court-yard, from the court-yard to the arched gateway, to speed the parting guest.

My lady's yellow curls flashed hither and thither like wandering gleams of sunshine on these busy days of farewell.   Her great blue eyes had a pretty mournful look, in charming unison with the soft pressure of her little hand, and that friendly, though perhaps rather stereotyped speech, in which she told her visitors how she was *so* sorry to lose them, and how she didn't know what she should do till they came once more to enliven the Court by their charming society.

But however sorry my lady might be to lose her visitors, there was at least one guest whose society she was not deprived of. Robert Audley showed no intention whatever of leaving his uncle's house. He had no professional duties, he said; Fig-tree Court was delightfully shady in hot weather, but there was a sharp corner round which the wind came in the winter months, armed with avenging rheumatisms and influenzas. Everybody was so good to him at the Court, that really he had no inclination to hurry away.

Sir Michael had but one answer to this: " Stay, my dear boy; stay, my dear Bob, as long as ever you like. I have no son, and you stand to me in the place of one. Make yourself agreeable to Lucy, and make the Court your home as long as you live."

To which Robert would merely reply by grasping his uncle's hand vehemently, and muttering something about " a jolly old prince."

It was to be observed that there was sometimes a certain vague sadness in the young man's tone when he called Sir Michael " a jolly old prince;"

some shadow of affectionate regret that brought a mist into Robert's eyes, as he sat in a corner of the room looking thoughtfully at the white-bearded baronet.

Before the last of the young sportsmen departed, Sir Harry Towers demanded and obtained an interview with Miss Alicia Audley in the oak library—an interview in which considerable emotion was displayed by the stalwart young fox-hunter; so much emotion, indeed, and of such a genuine and honest character, that Alicia fairly broke down as she told him that she should for ever esteem and respect him for his true and noble heart, but that he must never, never, never, unless he wished to cause her the most cruel distress, ask more from her than this esteem and respect.

Sir Harry left the library by the French window opening into the pond-garden. He strolled into that very lime-walk which George Talboys had compared to an avenue in a church-yard, and under the leafless trees fought the battle of his brave young heart.

"What a fool I am to feel it like this!" he cried, stamping his foot upon the frosty ground. "I always knew it would be so; I always knew that she was a hundred times too good for me. God bless her! How nobly and tenderly she spoke; how beautiful she looked with the crimson blushes under her brown skin, and the tears in her big grey eyes—almost as handsome as the day she took the sunk fence, and let me put the brush in her hat as we rode home! God bless her! I can get over anything as long as she doesn't care for that sneaking lawyer. But I couldn't stand that."

That sneaking lawyer, by which appellation Sir Harry alluded to Mr. Robert Audley, was standing in the hall, looking at a map of the midland counties, when Alicia came out of the library, with red eyes, after her interview with the fox-hunting baronet.

Robert, who was short-sighted, had his eyes within half an inch of the surface of the map as the young lady approached him.

"Yes," he said, "Norwich *is* in Norfolk, and

that fool, young Vincent, said it was in Hereford-
shire. Ha, Alicia, is that you ? "

He turned round so as to intercept Miss Audley
on her way to the staircase.

" Yes," replied his cousin curtly, trying to
pass him.

" Alicia, you've been crying ? "

The young lady did not condescend to
reply.

" You've been crying, Alicia. Sir Harry Towers,
of Towers Park, in the county of Herts, has been
making you an offer of his hand, eh ? "

" Have you been listening at the door, Mr.
Audley ?" .

" I have not, Miss Audley. On principle I
object to listen, and in practice I believe it to
be a very troublesome procceding; but I am a
barrister, Miss Alicia, and able to draw a conclusion by induction.   Do you know what induc-
tive evidence is, Miss Audley ? "

" No," replied Alicia, looking at her cousin as
a handsome young panther might look at its
daring tormentor.

"I thought not.　I dare say Sir Harry would ask if it was a new kind of horse-ball.　I knew by induction that the baronet was going to make you an offer; first, because he came down stairs with his hair parted on the wrong side, and his face as pale as the table-cloth; secondly, because he couldn't eat any breakfast, and let his coffee go the wrong way; and, thirdly, because he asked for an interview with you before he left the Court.　Well, how's it to be, Alicia?　Do you marry the baronet, and is poor Cousin Bob to be best man at the wedding?"

"Sir Harry Towers is a noble-hearted young man," said Alicia, still trying to pass her cousin.

"But do we accept him—yes or no?　Are we to be Lady Towers, with a superb estate in Hertfordshire, summer quarters for our hunters, and a drag with outriders to drive us across to papa's place in Essex?　Is it to be so, Alicia, or not?"

"What is that to you, Mr. Robert Audley?" cried Alicia passionately.　"What do *you* care what becomes of me, and whom I marry? If I married a chimney-sweep, you'd only lift up your eyebrows and say, ' Bless my soul, she was always eccentric.' I have refused Sir Harry Towers; but when I think of his generous and unselfish affection, and compare it with the heartless, lazy, selfish, supercilious indifference of other men, I've a good mind to run after him, and tell him—"

" That you'll retract, and be my Lady Towers?"

" Yes."

" Then don't, Alicia, don't," said Robert Audley, grasping his cousin's slender little wrist, and leading her upstairs. " Come into the drawing-room with me, Alicia, my poor little cousin; my charming, impetuous, alarming little cousin. Sit down here in this mullioned window, and let us talk seriously, and leave off quarrelling, if we can."

The cousins had the drawing-room all to themselves. Sir Michael was out, my lady in her own apartments, and poor Sir Harry Towers walking up and down upon the gravel walk, darkened with the flickering shadows of the leafless branches in the cold winter sunshine.

"My poor little Alicia," said Robert, as tenderly as if he had been addressing some spoiled child, "do you suppose that because people don't wear vinegar tops, or part their hair on the wrong side, or conduct themselves altogether after the manner of well-meaning maniacs, by way of proving the vehemence of their passion—do you suppose because of this, Alicia Audley, that they may not be just as sensible of the merits of a dear little, warm-hearted, and affectionate girl as ever their neighbours can be? Life is such a very troublesome matter, when all is said and done, that it's as well even to take its blessings quietly. I don't make a great howling because I can get good cigars one door from the corner of Chancery Lane, and have a dear, good girl for my cousin: but I am not the less grateful to Providence that it is so."

Alicia opened her grey eyes to their widest extent, looking her cousin full in the face with a bewildered stare. Robert had picked up the

ugliest and leanest of his attendant curs, and
was placidly stroking the animal's ears.

"Is this all you have to say to me, Robert?"
Miss Audley asked, meekly.

"Well, yes, I think so," replied her cousin,
after considerable deliberation. "I fancy that
what I wanted to say was this—don't marry the
fox-hunting baronet, if you like anybody else
better; for if you'll only be patient, and take life
easily, and try and reform yourself of banging
doors, bouncing in and out of rooms, talking of
the stables, and riding across country, I've no
doubt the person you prefer will make you a very
excellent husband."

"Thank you, cousin,' said Miss Audley,
crimsoning with bright indignant blushes up to
the roots of her waving brown hair; "but as you
may not know the person I prefer, I think you
had better not take upon yourself to answer for
him."

Robert pulled the dog's ears thoughtfully for
some moments.

"No, to be sure," he said, after a pause. "Of

course, if I don't know him—but I thought I
did."

" *Did you !* " exclaimed Alicia; and opening
the door with a violence that made her cousin
shiver, she bounced out of the drawing-room.

" I only said I thought I knew him," Robert
called after her; and then, as he sank into an
easy-chair, he murmured thoughtfully, " Such a
nice girl, too, if she didn't bounce!"

So poor Sir Harry Towers rode away from
Audley Court, looking very crestfallen and dismal.

He had very little pleasure now in returning
to the stately mansion hidden among sheltering
oaks and venerable beeches. The square, red-
brick house gleaming at the end of a long arcade
of leafless trees was to be for ever desolate, he
thought, since Alicia would not come to be its
mistress.

A hundred improvements planned and thought
of were dismissed from his mind as useless now.
The hunter that Jim the trainer was breaking in
for a lady ; the two pointer pups that were being
reared for the next shooting season; the big

olack retriever that would have carried Alicia's parasol; the pavilion in the garden, disused since his mother's death, but which he had meant to have restored for Miss Audley—all these things were now so much vanity and vexation of spirit.

"What's the good of being rich, if one has no one to help spend one's money?" said the young baronet. "One only grows a selfish beggar, and takes to drinking too much port. It's a hard thing that a girl can refuse a true heart and such stables as we've got at the park. It unsettles a man somehow."

Indeed, this unlooked-for rejection had very much unsettled the few ideas which made up the small sum of the young baronet's mind.

He had been desperately in love with Alicia ever since the last hunting season, when he had met her at a county ball. His passion, cherished through the slow monotony of a summer, had broken out afresh in the merry winter months, and the young man's *mauvaise honte* alone had delayed the offer of his hand. But he had never for a moment supposed that he would be refused;

he was so used to the adulation of mothers
who had daughters to marry, and of even the
daughters themselves; he had been so accustomed to feel himself the leading personage in an
assembly, although half the wits of the age had
been there, and he could only say, " Haw, to be
sure ! " and " By Jove ! " he had been so spoiled
by the flatteries of bright eyes that had looked, or
seemed to look, the brighter when he drew near,
that without being possessed of one shadow of
personal vanity, he had yet come to think that
he had only to make an offer to the prettiest girl
in Essex, to behold himself immediately accepted.

" Yes," he would say complacently to some
admiring satellite, " I know I'm a good match,
and I know what makes the gals so civil. They're
very pretty, and they're very friendly to a fellow;
but I don't care about 'em. They're all alike—
they can only drop their eyes and say, ' Lor,
Sir Harry, and why do you call that curly
black dog a retriever ? ' or, ' Oh, Sir Harry,
and did the poor mare really sprain her pastern shoulder-blade ? ' I haven't got much

brains myself, I know," the baronet would add
deprecatingly; "and I don't want a strong-
minded woman, who writes books and wears
green spectacles; but, hang it! I like a girl who
knows what she's talking about."

So when Alicia said "No," or rather, made
that pretty speech about esteem and respect,
which well-bred young ladies substitute for the
obnoxious monosyllable, Sir Harry Towers felt
that the whole fabric of the future he had built
up so complacently was shivered into a heap of
dingy ruins.

Sir Michael grasped him warmly by the hand
just before the young man mounted his horse in
the courtyard.

"I'm very sorry, Towers," he said. "You're
as good a fellow as ever breathed, and would
have made my girl an excellent husband; but
you know there's a cousin, and I think that——"

"Don't say that, Sir Michael," interposed the
fox-hunter energetically. "I can get over anything but that. A fellow whose hand upon the
curb weighs half a ton (why, he pulled the Cava-

s 2

her's mouth to pieces, Sir, the day you let him
ride the horse); a fellow who turns his collars
down, and eats bread and marmalade! No, no,
Sir Michael; it's a queer world, but I can't
think that of Miss Audley. There must be some
one in the background, Sir: it can't be the
cousin."

Sir Michael shook his head as the rejected
suitor rode away.

"I don't know about that," he muttered.
"Bob's a good lad, and the girl might do worse;
but he hangs back, as if he didn't care for her.
There's some mystery—there's some mystery!"

The old baronet said this in that semi-
thoughtful tone with which we speak of other
people's affairs. The shadows of the early winter
twilight, gathering thickest under the low oak
ceiling of the hall, and the quaint curve of the
arched doorway, fell darkly round his handsome
head; but the light of his declining life, his
beautiful and beloved young wife, was near
him, and he could see no shadows when she
was by.

She came skipping through the hall to meet him, and shaking her golden ringlets, buried her bright head on her husband's breast.

"So the last of our visitors is gone, dear, and we're all alone," she said. "Isn't that nice?"

"Yes, darling," he answered fondly, stroking her bright hair.

"Except Mr. Robert Audley. How long is that nephew of yours going to stay here?"

"As long as he likes, my pet; he's always welcome," said the baronet; and then, as if remembering himself, he added tenderly, "but not unless his visit is agreeable to you, darling; not if his lazy habits, or his smoking, or his dogs, or anything about him, is displeasing to you."

Lady Audley pursed up her rosy lips, and looked thoughtfully at the ground.

"It isn't that," she said hesitatingly. "Mr. Audley is a very agreeable young man, and a very honourable young man; but you know, Sir Michael, I'm rather a young aunt for such a nephew, and——"

"And what, Lucy?" asked the baronet, fiercely.

"Poor Alicia is rather jealous of any attention Mr. Audley pays me, and—and—I think it would be better for her happiness if your nephew were to bring his visit to a close."

"He shall go to-night, Lucy!" exclaimed Sir Michael. "I've been a blind, neglectful fool not to have thought of this before. My lovely little darling, it was scarcely just to Bob to expose the poor lad to your fascinations. I know him to be as good and true-hearted a fellow as ever breathed, but—but—he shall go to-night."

"But you won't be too abrupt, dear! You won't be rude?"

"Rude! No, Lucy. I left him smoking in the lime-walk. I'll go and tell him that he must get out of the house in an hour."

So in that leafless avenue, under whose gloomy shade George Talboys had stood on that thunderous evening before the day of his disappearance. Sir Michael Audley told his nephew that

the Court was no home for him, and that my
lady was too young and pretty to accept the
attentions of a handsome nephew of eight-and-
twenty.

Robert only shrugged his shoulders and elevated his thick black eyebrows, as Sir Michael
delicately hinted all this.

"I *have* been attentive to my lady," he said.
"She interests me—strongly, strangely interests
me;" and then, with a change in his voice, and
an emotion not common to him, he turned to
the baronet, and grasping his hand, exclaimed—
"God forbid, my dear uncle, that I should ever
bring trouble upon such a noble heart as yours!
God forbid that the lightest shadow of dishonour
should ever fall upon your honoured head—least
of all through any agency of mine!"

The young man uttered these few words in
a broken and disjointed fashion in which Sir
Michael had never heard him speak before, and
then, turning away his head, fairly broke down.

He left the Court that night, but he did not go
far. Instead of taking the evening train for

London, he went straight up to the little village
of Mount Stanning, and walking into the neatly-
kept inn, asked Phœbe Marks if he could be
accommodated with apartments.

CHAPTER XVII.

AT THE CASTLE INN.

THE little sitting-room into which Phœbe
Marks ushered the baronet's nephew was situated
on the ground floor, and only separated by a lath-
and-plaster partition from the little bar-parlour
occupied by the innkeeper and his wife.

It seemed as though the wise architect who had
superintended the building of the Castle Inn had
taken especial care that nothing but the frailest
and most flimsy material should be employed in
its construction, and that the wind, having a
special fancy for this unprotected spot, should
have full play for the indulgence of its caprices.

To this end pitiful woodwork had been used
instead of solid masonry; rickety ceilings had
been propped up by fragile rafters, and beams that
threatened on every stormy night to fall upon the
heads of those beneath them; doors whose spo-

ciality was never to be shut, yet always to be banging; windows constructed with a peculiar view to letting in the draught when they were closed, and keeping out the air when they were open. The hand of genius had devised this lonely country inn; and there was not an inch of wood-work, or a trowelful of plaster employed in all the rickety construction, that did not offer its own peculiar weak point to every assault of its inde-fatigable foe.

Robert looked about him with a feeble smile of resignation.

It was a change, decidedly, from the luxurious comforts of Audley Court, and it was rather a strange fancy of the young barrister to prefer loitering at this dreary village hostelry, to returning to his snug chambers in Fig-tree Court.

But he had brought his Lares and Penates with him, in the shape of his German pipe, his tobacco canister, half a dozen French novels, and his two ill-conditioned canine favourites, who sat shivering before the smoky little fire, barking shortly and sharply now and then, by way of hinting for some slight refreshment.

While Mr. Robert Audley contemplated his new quarters, Phœbe Marks summoned a little village lad who was in the habit of running errands for her, and taking him into the kitchen, gave him a tiny note, carefully folded and sealed.

"You know Audley Court?"

"Yes, Mum."

"If you'll run there with this letter to-night, and see that it's put safely into Lady Audley's hands, I'll give you a shilling."

"Yes, Mum."

"You understand? Ask to see my lady; you can say you've a message—not a note, mind—but a message from Phœbe Marks; and when you see her give this into her own hand."

"Yes, Mum."

"You, won't forget?"

"No, Mum."

"Then be off with you."

The boy waited for no second bidding, but in another moment was scudding along the hilly

high road, down the sharp descent that led to
Audley.

Phœbe Marks went to the window, and looked
out at the black figure of the lad hurrying through
the dusky winter evening.

"If there's any bad meaning in his comng
here," she thought, "my lady will know of it in
time, at any rate."

Phœbe herself brought the neatly-arranged tea-
tray; and the little covered dish of ham and eggs
which had been prepared for this unlooked-for
visitor. Her pale hair was as smoothly braided,
and her light grey dress fitted as precisely, as of
old. The same neutral tints pervaded her person
and her dress; no showy rose-coloured ribbons or
rustling silk gown proclaimed the well-to-do innkeeper's wife. Phœbe Marks was a person who
never lost her individuality. Silent and self-con-
tained, she seemed to hold herself within herself,
and take no colour from the outer world.

Robert looked at her thoughtfully as she spread
the cloth, and drew the table nearer to the fire-
place.

"That," he thought, "is a woman who could keep a secret."

The dogs looked rather suspiciously at the quiet figure of Mrs. Marks gliding softly about the room, from the teapot to the caddy, and from the caddy to the kettle singing on the hob.

"Will you pour out my tea for me, Mrs. Marks?" said Robert, seating himself in a horse-hair-covered arm-chair, which fitted him as tightly in every direction as if he had been measured for it.

"You have come straight from the Court, Sir?" said Phœbe, as she handed Robert the sugar-basin.

"Yes; I only left my uncle's an hour ago."

"And my lady, Sir, was she quite well?"

"Yes, quite well."

"As gay and light-hearted as ever, Sir?"

"As gay and light-hearted as ever."

Phœbe retired respectfully after having given Mr. Audley his tea, but as she stood with her hand upon the lock of the door he spoke again.

"You knew Lady Audley when she was Miss Lucy Graham, did you not?" he asked.

"Yes, Sir. I lived at Mrs. Dawson's when my lady was governess there."

"Indeed! Was she long in the surgeon's family?"

"A year and a half, Sir."

"And she came from London?"

"Yes, Sir."

"And she was an orphan, I believe?"

"Yes, Sir."

"Always as cheerful as she is now?"

"Always, Sir."

Robert emptied his teacup and handed it to Mrs. Marks. Their eyes met—a lazy look in his, and an active, searching glance in hers.

"This woman would be good in a witness-box," he thought; "it would take a clever lawyer to bother her in a cross-examination."

He finished his second cup of tea, pushed away his plate, fed his dogs, and lighted his pipe, while Phœbe carried off the tea-tray.

The wind came whistling up across the frosty

open country, and through the leafless woods, and
ráttled fiercely at the window-frames.

"There's a triangular draught from those two
windows and the door that scarcely adds to the
comfort of this apartment," murmured Robert;
"and there certainly are pleasanter sensations
than that of standing up to one's knees in cold
water."

He poked the fire, patted his dogs, put on his
great-coat, rolled a rickety old sofa close to the
hearth, wrapped his legs in his railway rug, and
stretching himself at full length upon the narrow
horsehair cushion, smoked his pipe, and watched
the bluish-grey wreaths curling slowly upwards to
the dingy ceiling.

"No," he murmured again; "that is a woman
who can keep a secret. A counsel for the prose-
cution would get very little out of her."

I have said that the bar-parlour was only separated from the sitting-room occupied by Robert
by a lath-and-plaster partition. The young barrister could hear the two or three village trades-
men and a couple of farmers laughing and talking

round the bar, while Luke Marks served them from his stock of liquors.

Very often he could even hear their words, especially the landlord's, for he spoke in a coarse, loud voice, and had a more boastful manner than any of his customers.

"The man is a fool," said Robert, as he laid down his pipe. "I'll go and talk to him by-and-by."

He waited till the few visitors to the Castle had dropped away one by one, and, when Luke Marks had bolted the front door upon the last of his customers, he strolled quietly into the bar-parlour where the landlord was seated with his wife.

Phœbe was busy at a little table, upon which stood a prim workbox, with every reel of cotton and glistening steel bodkin in its appointed place. She was darning the coarse grey stockings that adorned her husband's awkward feet, but she did her work as daintily as if they had been my lady's delicate silken hose.

I say that she took no colour from external things, and that the vague air of refinement that pervaded her nature, clung to her as closely in the society of her boorish husband at the Castle Inn, as in Lady Audley's fairy boudoir at the Court.

She looked up suddenly as Robert entered the bar-parlour. There was some shade of vexation in her pale grey eyes, which changed to an expression of anxiety—nay, rather, of almost terror —as she glanced from Mr. Audley to Luke Marks.

"I have come in for a few minutes' chat before I go to bed," said Robert, settling himself very comfortably before the cheerful fire. "Would you object to a cigar, Mrs. Marks? I mean, of course, to my smoking one," he added, explanatorily.

"Not at all, Sir."

"It would be a good 'un her objectin' to a bit o' bacca," growled Mr. Marks, "when me and the customers smokes all day."

Robert lighted his cigar with a gilt-paper match of Phœbe's making that adorned the chimney-piece, and took half a dozen reflective puffs before he spoke.

"I want you to tell me all about Mount Stanning, Mr. Marks," he said presently.

"Then that's pretty soon told," replied Luke,
with a harsh, grating laugh. "Of all the dull
holes as ever a man set foot in, this is about the
dullest. Not that the business don't pay pretty
tidy; I don't complain of that; but I should ha'
liked a public at Chelmsford, or Brentwood, or
Romford, or some place where there's a bit of life
in the streets; and I might have had it," he
added, discontentedly, "if folks hadn't been so
precious stingy."

As her husband muttered this complaint in a
grumbling under-tone, Phœbe looked up from
her work and spoke to him.

"We forgot the brewhouse door, Luke," she
said. "Will you come with me and help me put
up the bar?"

"The brewhouse door can bide for to-night,"
said Mr. Marks; "I ain't agoin' to move now
I've seated myself for a comfortable smoke."

He took a long clay pipe from a corner of the
fender as he spoke, and began to fill it deliberately.

"I don't feel easy about that brewhouse door, Luke," remonstrated his wife; "there are always tramps about, and they can get in easily when the bar isn't up."

"Go and put the bar up yourself, then, can't you!" answered Mr. Marks.

"It's too heavy for me to lift."

"Then let it bide, if you're too fine a lady to see to it yourself. You're very anxious all of a sudden about this here brewhouse door. I suppose you don't want me to open my mouth to this gent, that's about it. Oh, you needn't frown at me to stop my speaking! You're always putting in your tongue and clipping off my words before I've half said 'em; but I won't stand it. Do you hear? I won't stand it!"

Phœbe Marks shrugged her shoulders, folded her work, shut her workbox, and crossing her hands in her lap, sat with her grey eyes fixed upon her husband's bull-like face.

"Then you don't particularly care to live at Mount Stanning?" said Robert, politely, as if anxious to change the conversation."

T 2

"No, I don't," answered Luke; "and I don't care who knows it; and, as I said before, if folks hadn't been so precious stingy, I might have had a public in a thrivin' market town, instead of this tumble-down old place, where a man has his hair blowed off his head on a windy day. What's fifty pound, or what's a hundred pound——?"

"Luke! Luke!"

"No, you're not agoin' to stop my mouth with all your 'Luke, Lukes!'" answered Mr. Marks, to his wife's remonstrance. "I say again, what's a hundred pound?"

"No, answered Robert Audley, 'speaking with wonderful distinctness, and addressing his words to Luke Marks, but fixing his eyes upon Phœbe's anxious face. "What, indeed, is a hundred pounds to a man possessed of the power which you hold, or rather which your wife holds, over the person in question?"

Phœbe's face, at all times almost colourless, seemed scarcely capable of growing paler; but as her eyelids dropped under Robert Audley's searching glance, a visible change came over the pallid hues of her complexion.

"A quarter to twelve," said Robert, looking at his watch. " Late hours for such a quiet village as Mount Stanning. Good night, my worthy host. Good night, Mrs. Marks. You needn't send me my shaving water till nine o'clock to-morrow morning."

CHAPTER XVIII.

ROBERT RECEIVES A VISITOR WHOM HE HAD SCARCELY EXPECTED.

ELEVEN o'clock struck the next morning, and found Mr. Robert Audley still lounging over the well-ordered little breakfast table, with one of his dogs at each side of his arm-chair, regarding him with watchful eyes and opened mouth, awaiting the expected morsel of ham or toast. Robert had a county paper on his knees, and made a feeble effort now and then to read the first page, which was filled with advertisements of farming stock, quack medicines, and other interesting matter.

The weather had changed, and the snow, which had for the last few days been looming blackly in the frosty sky, fell in great feathery flakes against the windows, and lay piled in the little bit of garden ground without.

The long, lonely road leading towards Audley

seemed untrodden by a footstep, as Robert looked out at the wintry landscape.

"Lively," he said, "for a man used to the fascinations of Temple Bar!"

As he watched the snow-flakes falling every moment thicker and faster upon the lonely road, he was surprised by seeing a brougham driving slowly up the hill.

"I wonder what unhappy wretch has too restless a spirit to stop at home on such a morning as this," he muttered, as he returned to the armchair by the fire.

He had only reseated himself a few minutes when Phœbe Marks entered the room to announce Lady Audley.

"Lady Audley! Pray beg her to come in," said Robert; and then, as Phœbe left the room to usher in this unexpected visitor, he muttered between his teeth—

"A false move, my lady, and one I never looked for from you."

Lucy Audley was radiant on this cold and snowy January morning. Other people's noses are rudely assailed by the sharp fingers of the grim ice-king, but not my lady's; other people's lips turn pale and blue with the chilling influence of the bitter weather, but my lady's pretty little rosebud of a mouth retained its brightest colouring and cheeriest freshness.

She was wrapped in the very sables which Robert Audley had brought from Russia, and carried a muff that the young man thought seemed almost as big as herself.

She looked a childish, helpless, babyfied little creature; and Robert watched her with some touch of pity in his eyes, as she came up to the hearth by which he was standing, and warmed her tiny gloved hands at the blaze.

"What a morning, Mr. Audley," she said, "what a morning!"

"Yes, indeed! Why did you come out in such weather, Lady Audley?"

"Because I wished to see you—particularly."

"Indeed!"

"Yes," said my lady, with an air of considerable embarrassment, playing with the button of her glove, and almost wrenching it off in her restlessness—"yes, Mr. Audley, I felt that you had not been well treated; that—that you had, in short, reason to complain; and that an apology was due to you."

"I do not wish for any apology, Lady Audley."

"But you are entitled to one," answered my lady, quietly. "Why, my dear Robert, should we be so very ceremonious towards each other? You were very comfortable at Audley; we were very glad to have you there; but my dear, silly husband must needs take it into his foolish head that it is dangerous for his poor little wife's peace of mind to have a nephew of eight or nine-and-twenty smoking his cigars in her boudoir, and, behold! our pleasant little family circle is broken up."

Lucy Audley spoke with that peculiar childish vivacity which seemed so natural to her. Robert looked down almost sadly at her bright, animated face.

"Lady Audley," he said, "Heaven forbid that either you or I should ever bring grief or dishonour upon my uncle's generous heart! Better perhaps, that I should be out of the house—better, perhaps, that I had never entered it ! "

My lady had been looking at the fire while her nephew spoke, but at his last words she lifted her head suddenly, and looked him full in the face with a wondering expression—an earnest, questioning gaze, whose full meaning the young barrister understood.

"Oh, pray do not be alarmed, Lady Audley," he said gravely. "You have no sentimental nonsense, no silly infatuation, borrowed from Balzac, or Dumas *fils*, to fear from me. The benchers of the Inner Temple will tell you that Robert Audley is troubled with none of the epidemics whose outward signs are turn-down collars and Byronic neckties. I say that I wish I had never entered my uncle's house during the last year; but I say it with a far more solemn meaning than any sentimental one."

My lady shrugged her shoulders.

"If you insist on talking in enigmas, Mr. Audley," she said, "you must forgive a poor little woman if she declines to answer them."

Robert made no reply to this speech.

"But tell me," said my lady, with an entire change of tone, "what could have induced you to come up to this dismal place?"

"Curiosity."

"Curiosity!"

"Yes; I felt an interest in that bull-necked man, with the dark red hair and wicked grey eyes. A dangerous man, my lady—a man in whose power I should not like to be."

A sudden change came over Lady Audley's face; the pretty roseate flush faded out from her cheeks, and left them waxen white, and angry flashes lightened in her blue eyes.

"What have I done to you, Robert Audley," she cried passionately—"what have I done to you, that you should hate me so?"

He answered her very gravely,—

"I had a friend, Lady Audley, whom I loved very dearly, and since I have lost him I fear that my feelings towards other people are strangely embittered."

"You mean—the Mr. Talboys who went to Australia?"

"Yes, I mean the Mr. Talboys, who I was told set out for Liverpool with the idea of going to Australia."

"And you do not believe in his having sailed for Australia?"

"I do not."

"But why not?"

"Forgive me, Lady Audley, if I decline to answer that question."

"As you please," she said carelessly.

"A week after my friend disappeared, continued Robert, "I posted an advertisement to the Sydney and Melbourne papers, calling upon him, if he was in either city when the advertisement appeared, to write and tell me of his whereabouts, and also calling on any one who had met him, either in the colonies or on the voyage out, to give me any information respecting him. George Talboys left Essex, or disappeared from Essex, on the 6th of September last. I ought to receive some answer to this advertisment by the end of

this month. To-day is the 27th: the time draws
very near."

"And if you receive no answer?" asked Lady
Audley.

"If I receive no answer I shall think that my
fears have been not unfounded, and I shall do my
best to act."

"What do you mean by that?"

"Ah, Lady Audley, you remind me how very
powerless I am in this matter. My friend might
have been made away with in this very inn,
stabbed to death upon this hearth-stone on which
I now stand, and I might stay here for a twelvemonth, and go away at the last as ignorant of his
fate as if I had never crossed the threshold.
What do we know of the mysteries that may hang
about the houses we enter! If I were to go to-
morrow into that common-place, plebeian, eight-
roomed house in which Maria Manning and her
husband murdered their guest, I should have no
awful prescience of that bygone horror. Foul
deeds have been done under the most hospitable
roofs, terrible crimes have been committed amid

the fairest scenes, and have left no trace upon the spot where they were done. I do not believe in mandrake, or in blood-stains that no time can efface. I believe rather that we may walk unconsciously in an atmosphere of crime, and breathe none the less freely. I believe that we may look into the smiling face of a murderer, and admire its tranquil beauty."

My lady laughed at Robert's earnestness.

"You seem to have quite a taste for discussing these horrible subjects," she said, rather scornfully; "you ought to have been a detective police officer."

"I sometimes think I should have been a good one."

"Why?"

"Because I am patient."

"But to return to Mr. George Talboys, whom we lost sight of in your eloquent discussion. What if you receive no answer to your advertisements?"

"I shall then consider myself justified in concluding that my friend is dead."

"Yes, and then ——— ? "

" I shall examine the effects he left at my chambers."

" Indeed! and what are they? Coats, waist-coats, varnished boots, and meerschaum pipes, I suppose," said Lady Audley, laughing.

" No; letters—letters from his friends, his old school-fellows, his father, his brother-officers."

" Yes ? "

" Letters, too, from his wife."

My lady was silent for some few moments, look-ing thoughtfully at the fire.

" Have you ever seen any of the letters written by the late Mrs. Talboys ? " she asked presently.

" Never. Poor soul! her letters are not likely to throw much light upon my friend's fate. I dare say she wrote the usual womanly scrawl. There are very few who write so charming and uncommon a hand as yours, Lady Audley."

" Ah, you know my hand of course."

"Yes, I know it very well, indeed."

My lady warmed her hands once more, and then taking up the big muff which she had laid aside upon a chair, prepared to take her departure.

"You have refused to accept my apology, Mr. Audley," she said; "but I trust you are not the less assured of my feelings towards you."

"Perfectly assured, Lady Audley."

"Then good-by, and let me recommend you not to stay long in this miserable draughty place, if you do not wish to take rheumatism back to Fig-tree Court."

"I shall return to town to-morrow morning to see after my letters."

"Then, once more, good-by."

She held out her hand; he took it loosely in his own. It seemed such a feeble little hand that he might have crushed it in his strong grasp, had he chosen to be so pitiless.

He attended her to her carriage, and watched it as it drove off, not towards Audley, but in the direction of Brentwood, which was about six miles from Mount Stanning.

About an hour and a half after this, as Robert stood at the door of the inn, smoking a cigar and watching the snow falling in the whitened fields opposite, he saw the brougham drive back, empty this time, to the door of the inn.

" Have you taken Lady Audley back to the Court? " he said to the coachman, who had stopped to call for a mug of hot spiced ale.

" No, Sir; I've just come from the Brentwood station. My lady started for London by the 12·40 train."

" For town? "

" Yes, Sir."

" My lady gone to London ! " said Robert, as he returned to the little sitting-room.   " Then I'll follow her by the next train; and if I'm not very much mistaken, I know where to find her.'·

He packed his portmanteau, paid his bill, which was carefully receipted by Phœbe Marks, fastened his dogs together with a couple of leathern collars and a chain, and stepped into the rumbling fly kept at the Castle Inn for the convenience of Mount Stanning.   He caught an express that left Brentwood at three o'clock, and settled himself comfortably in a corner of an empty first-class carriage, coiled up in a couple of huge railway rugs, and smoking a cigar in mild defiance of the authorities. "The Company may make as many bye-laws as they please," he murmured, "but I shall take the liberty of enjoying my cheroot as long as I've half-a-crown left to give the guard."

CHAPTER XIX.

THE BLACKSMITH'S MISTAKE.

IT was exactly five minutes past four as Mr.
Robert Audley stepped out upon the platform at
Shoreditch, and waited placidly until such time as
his dogs and his portmanteau should be delivered
up to the attendant porter who had called his cab,
and undertaken the general conduct of his affairs,
with that disinterested courtesy which does such
infinite credit to a class of servitors who are for-
bidden to accept the tribute of a grateful public.
Robert Audley waited with consummate patience
for a considerable time; but as the express was
generally a long train, and as there were a great
many passengers from Norfolk carrying guns and
pointers, and other paraphernalia of a critical description, it took a long while to make matters
agreeable to all claimants, and even the barrister's

seraphic indifference to mundane affairs nearly gave way.

" Perhaps, when that gentleman who is making such a noise about a pointer with liver-coloured spots, has discovered the particular pointer and spots that he wants—which happy combination of events scarcely seems likely to arrive—they'll give me my luggage and let me go. The designing wretches knew at a glance that I was born to be imposed upon; and that if they were to trample the life out of me upon this very platform, I should never have the spirit to bring an action against the Company." Suddenly an idea seemed to strike him, and he left the porter to struggle for the custody of his goods, and walked round to the other side of the station.

He had heard a bell ring, and, looking at the clock, had remembered that the down-train for Colchester started at this time. He had learned what it was to have an honest purpose since the disappearance of George Talboys; and he reached the opposite platform in time to see the passengers take their seats.

There was one lady who had evidently only just arrived at the station; for she hurried on to the platform at the very moment that Robert approached the train, and almost ran against that gentleman in her haste and excitement.

"I beg your pardon——" she began, ceremoniously; then raising her eyes from Mr. Audley's waistcoat, which was about on a level with her pretty face, she exclaimed, "Robert! You in London already?"

"Yes, Lady Audley; you were quite right, the Castle Inn is a dismal place, and——"

"You got tired of it—I knew you would. Please open the carriage-door for me: the train will start in two minutes."

Robert Audley was looking at his uncle's wife with rather a puzzled expression of countenance.

"What does it mean?" he thought. "She is altogether a different being to the wretched, helpless creature who dropped her mask for a moment, and looked at me with her own pitiful face, in the little room at Mount Stanning, four hours ago. What has happened to cause the change?"

He opened the door for her while he thought this, and helped her to settle herself in her seat, spreading her furs over her knees, and arranging the huge velvet mantle in which her slender little figure was almost hidden.

"Thank you very much; how good you are to me!" she said, as he did this. "You will think me very foolish to travel upon such a day, without my dear darling's knowledge too; but I went up to · town to settle a very terrific milliner's bill, which I did not wish my best of husbands to see; for indulgent as he is, he might think me extravagant; and I cannot bear to suffer even in his thoughts."

"Heaven forbid that you ever should, Lady Audley," Robert said, gravely.

She looked at him for a moment with a smile, which had something defiant in its brightness.

"Heaven forbid it, indeed," she murmured. "I don't think I ever shall."

The second bell rang, and the train moved as she spoke. The last Robert Audley saw of her was that bright defiant smile.

"Whatever object brought her to London has

been successfully accomplished," he thought. "Has she baffled me by some piece of womanly jugglery? Am I never to get any nearer to the truth; but am I to be tormented all my life by vague doubts, and wretched suspicions, which may grow upon me till I become a monomaniac? Why did she come to London?"

He was still mentally asking himself this question as he ascended the stairs in Fig-tree Court, with one of his dogs under each arm, and his railway rugs over his shoulder.

He found his chambers in their accustomed order. The geraniums had been carefully tended, and the canaries had retired for the night under cover of a square of green baize, testifying to the care of honest Mrs. Maloney. Robert cast a hurried glance round the sitting-room; then setting down the dogs upon the hearth-rug, he walked straight into the little inner chamber which served as his dressing-room.

It was in this room that he kept disused portmanteaus, battered japanned cases, and other lumber; and it was in this room that George

Talboys had left his luggage. Robert lifted a portmanteau from the top of a large trunk, and kneeling down before it with a lighted candle in his hand, carefully examined the lock.

To all appearance it was exactly in the same condition in which George had left it when he laid his mourning garments aside and placed them in this shabby repository, with all other memorials of his dead wife. Robert brushed his coat sleeve across the worn leather-covered lid, upon which the initials G. T. were inscribed with big brass-headed nails; but Mrs. Maloney, the laundress, must have been the most precise of housewives, for neither the portmanteau nor the trunk were dusty.

Mr. Audley despatched a boy to fetch his Irish attendant, and paced up and down his sitting-room, waiting anxiously for her arrival.

She came in about ten minutes, and, after expressing her delight in the return of "the masther," humbly awaited his orders.

"I only sent for you to ask if anybody has been here; that is to say, if anybody has

applied to you for the key of my rooms to-day—
any lady ? "

" Lady ? No, indeed, yer honour; there's been
no lady for the kay; barrin' it's the blacksmith
yer honour manes."

" The blacksmith ! "

" Yes; the blacksmith your honour ordered to
come to-day."

"I order a blacksmith!" exclaimed Robert, "I
left a bottle of French brandy in the cupboard,"
he thought, "and Mrs. M. has been evidently
enjoying herself."

" Sure, and the blacksmith your honour tould
to see to the locks," replied Mrs. Maloney. " It's
him that lives down in one of the little streets
by the bridge," she added, giving a very lucid
description of the man's whereabouts.

Robert lifted his eyebrows in mute despair.

" If you'll sit down and compose yourself, Mrs.
M.," he said—he abbreviated her name thus on
principle, for the avoidance of unnecessary labour—
"perhaps we shall be able by-and-by to understand
each other. You say a blacksmith has been here ? "

"Sure and I did, sir."

"To-day?"

"Quite correct, sir."

Step by step Mr. Audley elicited the following information. A locksmith had called upon Mrs. Maloney that afternoon at three o'clock, and had asked for the key of Mr. Audley's chambers; in order that he might look to the locks of the doors, which he stated were all out of repair. He declared that he was acting upon Mr. Audley's own orders, conveyed to him by a letter from the country, where the gentleman was spending his Christmas. Mrs. Maloney, believing in the truth of this statement, had admitted the man to the chambers, where he stayed about half an hour.

"But you were with him while he examined the locks, I suppose?" Mr. Audley asked.

"Sure I was, sir, in and out, as you may say, all the time; for I've been cleaning the stairs this afternoon, and I took the opporchunity to begin my scouring while the man was at work."

"Oh, you were in and out all the time. It you *could* conveniently give me a plain answer,

Mrs. M., I should be glad to know what was the longest time that you were *out* while the locksmith was in my chambers?"

But Mrs. Maloney could not give a plain answer. It might have been ten minutes; though she didn't think it was as much. It might have been a quarter of an hour; but she was sure it wasn't more. It didn't *seem* to her more than five minutes; but "thim stairrs, your honour—" and here she rambled off into a disquisition upon the scouring of stairs in general, and the stairs outside Robert's chambers in particular.

Mr. Audley sighed the weary sigh of mournful resignation.

"Never mind, Mrs. M.," he said; "the locksmith had plenty of time to do anything he wanted to do, I daresay, without your being any the wiser."

Mrs. Maloney stared at her employer with mingled surprise and alarm.

"Sure, there wasn't anythin' for him to stale, your honour, barrin' the birrds and the geranums, and——"

"No, no, I understand. There, that'll do, Mrs. M. Tell me where the man lives, and I'll go and see him."

"But you'll have a bit of dinner first, sir?"

"I'll go and see the locksmith before I have my dinner."

He took up his hat as he announced his determination, and walked towards the door.

"The man's address, Mrs. M.?"

The Irishwoman directed him to a small street at the back of St. Bride's Church, and thither Mr. Robert Audley quietly strolled, through the miry slush which simple Londoners call *snow*.

He found the locksmith, and, at the sacrifice of the crown of his hat, contrived to enter the low narrow doorway of a little open shop. A jet of gas was flaring in the unglazed window, and there was a very merry party in the little room behind the shop; but no one responded to Robert's "Hulloa!" The reason of this was sufficiently obvious. This merry party was so much absorbed in its own merriment as to be deaf to all com-

mon-place summonses from the outer world; and
it was only when Robert, advancing further into
the cavernous little shop, made so bold as to open
the half-glass door which separated him from the
merry-makers, that he succeeded in obtaining their
attention.

A very jovial picture of the Teniers school was
presented to Mr. Robert Audley upon the opening
of this door.

The locksmith, with his wife and family, and
two or three droppers-in of the female sex, were
clustered about a table, which was adorned by
two bottles : not vulgar bottles of that colourless
extract of the juniper berry, much affected by
the masses; but of *bond fide* port and sherry—
fiercely strong sherry, which left a fiery taste in
the mouth ; nut-brown sherry—rather unnaturally
brown, if anything—and fine old port; no sickly
vintage, faded and thin from excessive age ; but a
rich, full-bodied wine, sweet and substantial, and
high coloured.

The locksmith was speaking as Robert Audley
opened the door.

"And with that," he said, "she walked off, as graceful as you please."

The whole party was thrown into confusion by the appearance of Mr. Audley; but it was to be observed that the locksmith was more embarrassed than his companions. He set down his glass so hurriedly, that he spilt his wine, and wiped his mouth nervously with the back of his dirty hand.

"You called at my chambers to-day," Robert said, quietly. "Don't let me disturb you, ladies." This to the droppers-in. "You called at my chambers to-day, Mr. White, and——"

The man interrupted him.

"I hope, sir, you'll be so good as to look over the mistake," he stammered. "I'm sure, sir, I'm very sorry it should have occurred. I was sent for to another gentleman's chambers, Mr. Aulwin, in Garden-court; and the name slipped my memory; and havin' done odd jobs before for you, I thought it must be you as wanted me to-day; and I called at Mrs. Maloney's for the key accordin'; but directly I see the locks in your chambers, I says to myself, 'the gentleman's locks ain't out of order; the gentleman don't want all his locks repaired.' "

" But you stayed half an hour."

" Yes, sir; for there was *one* lock out of order— the door nighest the staircase—and I took it off and cleaned it, and put it on again. I won't charge you nothin' for the job, and I hope as you'll be so good as to look over the mistake as has occurred, which I've been in business thirteen year come July, and——"

" Nothing of this kind ever happened before, I suppose," said Robert, gravely. " No, it's altogether a singular kind of business, not likely to come about every day. You've been enjoying yourself this evening, I see, Mr. White. You've done a good stroke of work to-day, I'll wager— made a lucky hit, and you're what you call ' standing treat,' eh ?"

Robert Audley looked straight into the man's dingy face as he spoke. The locksmith was not a bad-looking fellow, and there was nothing that he need have been ashamed of in his face, except the dirt, and that, as Hamlet's mother says, "is common;" but in spite of this, Mr. White's eyelids dropped under the young barrister's calm scrutiny, and he stammered out some apologetic sort of speech about his "missus," and his missus's neighbours, and port wine and sherry wine, with as much confusion as if he, an honest mechanic in a free country, were called upon to excuse himself to Mr. Robert Audley for being caught in the act of enjoying himself in his own parlour.

Robert cut him short with a careless nod.

"Pray don't apologise," he said; "I like to see people enjoy themselves. Good night, Mr. White —good night, ladies."

He lifted his hat to "the missus," and the missus's neighbours, who were much fascinated by his easy manner and his handsome face, and left the shop.

"And so," he muttered to himself as he went back to his chambers, "'with that she walked off as graceful as you please.' Who was it that walked off? and what was the story which the locksmith was telling when I interrupted him at that sentence? Oh, George Talboys, George Talboys, am I ever to come any nearer to the secret of your fate? Am I coming nearer to it now, slowly but surely? Is the radius to grow narrower day by day, until it draws a dark circle round the home of those I love? How is it all to end?"

He sighed wearily as he walked slowly back across the flagged quadrangles in the Temple to his own solitary chambers.

Mrs. Maloney had prepared for him that bachelor's dinner which, however excellent and nutritious in itself, has no claim to the special charm of novelty. She had cooked for him a mutton chop, which was soddening itself between two plates upon the little table near the fire.

Robert Audley sighed as he sat down to the familiar meal; remembering his uncle's cook with a fond, regretful sorrow.

" Her cutlets à la Maintenon made mutton seem more than mutton; a sublimated meat that could scarcely have grown upon any mundane sheep," he murmured, sentimentally, "and Mrs. Maloney's chops are apt to be tough; but such is life—what does it matter?"

He pushed away his plate impatiently after eating a few mouthfuls.

"I have never eaten a good dinner at this table since I lost George Talboys," he said. "The place seems as gloomy as if the poor fellow had died in the next room, and had never been taken away to be buried. How long ago that September afternoon appears as I look back at it—that September afternoon upon which I parted with him alive and well; and lost him as suddenly and unaccountably as if a trap-door had opened in the solid earth, and let him through to the Antipodes!"

END OF VOL. I.

BRADBURY AND EVANS, PRINTERS, WHITEFRIARS.

TINSLEY BROTHERS'
LIST OF NEW WORKS.

Ready this day at every Library, in Three Volumes, post 8vo,

LADY AUDLEY'S SECRET.

BY M. E. BRADDON,

Author of "Aurora Floyd."

Dedicated by Special Permission to Sir Edward Lytton Bulwer, Bart., M.P.

Now Ready at all Libraries, in One Volume, 8vo,

THE PUBLIC

LIFE OF LORD MACAULAY.

BY FREDERICK ARNOLD, B.A.,

Of Christ Church, Oxford.

"This 'Public Life of Lord Macaulay' is rendered more valuable from the citations which, with very few exceptions, have been taken from writings unknown or practically inaccessible to the general reader ; and the author has rescued from possible oblivion some important fragments, interesting for their intrinsic merit and their biographical value."—*Observer.*

MR. SALA'S NEW WORK.

Now Ready, in One Volume, Post 8vo,

ACCEPTED ADDRESSES.

BY GEORGE AUGUSTUS SALA,

Author of the "Seven Sons of Mammon," "Dutch Pictures," &c.

Now Ready at all Libraries, in Two Volumes,

THE LITERATURE OF SOCIETY.

BY GRACE WHARTON,

One of the Authors of "The Queens of Society," &c.

Now Ready,

UNIFORM WITH THE "LITTLE TOUR IN IRELAND,"

With Illustrations by CHARLES KEENE, *price 6s.,*

THE CAMBRIDGE GRISETTE.
BY HERBERT VAUGHAN.

Now Ready, in Two Small Volumes,

DANTE'S DIVINA COMMEDIA.
TRANSLATED INTO ENGLISH IN THE METRE AND TRIPLE RHYME OF THE ORIGINAL,
BY MRS. RAMSAY.

In Three Parts.   Parts I. and II. now ready, neatly bound in green cloth.

Now Ready at every Library, a New Novel, in Two Volumes, entitled

TWO LIVES.
BY BLANCHARD JERROLD.

Now Ready at every Library, in One Volume,

CHATEAU FRISSAC;
OR, HOME SCENES IN FRANCE.

BY THE AUTHOR OF "PHOTOGRAPHS OF PARIS LIFE."

"'Château Frissac' is a pleasant novellette, wittily written, and intended to show the evils of *Mariages de Convenance*.   The authoress is both humorous and witty.   Wit abounds in both colloquy and anecdote."—*Press.*

"There is a delightful vivacity and an ease in many of the conversational scenes with which this novellette abounds which are eminently French.   While reading the pages of 'Chroniqueuse,' we might almost fancy ourselves in one of the pleasantest of the Parisian *salons ;* and, although we cannot help feeling that the various human units introduced to our notice are individually by no means deserving of much sympathy, collectively we are bound to say they are for a time very amusing and pleasant company."—*The Critic.*

Now Ready, price 5s.,

DUTCH PICTURES.
WITH SOME SKETCHES IN THE FLEMISH MANNER.
BY GEORGE AUGUSTUS SALA.

"There is a genuine air of homespun earnestness about such a picture as the following which, though it might have been written by Dickens, has more in it of Mr. Sala's personal bias."—*Spectator.*

CPSIA information can be obtained at www.ICGtesting.com
Printed in the USA
BVOW05s1408020316

438803BV00012B/58/P